NEGOTIATING: EVERYBODY WINS

VANESSA HELPS

BBC BOOKS

Published by BBC Books
a division of BBC Enterprises Limited
Woodlands, 80 Wood Lane, London W12 0TT

First published 1992

Reprinted 1993

© Vanessa Helps 1992

ISBN 0 563 36289 8

Set in 10.5/12.5 Times Roman by Coda Consultants, Hampshire
Printed in England by Clays Ltd, St Ives plc
Cover printed by Clays Ltd, St Ives plc

Contents

The Author

Vanessa Helps, BA, MA, FIPM, has been an independent Human Resources Consultant and trainer in both the public and private sector for fourteen years. She specialises in developing equal opportunities and leadership for women and men managers. Previously she was a management developer, adviser and trainer in the financial sector and a staff manager in retailing. She is an associate of Ashridge Management College, and has run Negotiating Skills Programmes extensively over the past eight years, the product of which is in this book.

She lives on the south coast of England between the sea and the New Forest with her musician husband Dave Walters and their two young children, and she spends as much time as possible in, by or on the water.

Acknowledgements

Many people have enabled this book to be written and published:

The women and men who have attended the workshops on negotiating I have run over the past eight years, particularly those in publishing

Philip Hodgson and **Valerie Hammond** for opening the door and sowing the original seed.

Jennifer Jones of BBC Books for the invitation to write this book and for her reassurance and belief that I could do it.

Friends and family who asked and encouraged. They know who they are. My daughter who models the marvellous power of the young as well as providing me with some glorious examples of negotiating.

Wendi Batchelor, who transcribed my thinking with calmness, energy and commitment and **Bill Martin** for his speedy and creative artwork.

Two pieces of music sustained my writing: Vaughan Williams' 'The Lark Ascending' and 'Don't Give Up' by Peter Gabriel with Kate Bush.

The cartoon on page 73 is reproduced by permission of Punch. The poem on page 9 is by Natasha Josefowitz, published by Warner Books Inc., New York, 1983. To the unknown originators of examples used in this book, thank you.

Without **Dave Walters**, my partner, husband, friend and champion, this book would never have been completed. His energy, encouragement and patience combined with music and desktop publishing brilliance all helped to transform these thoughts into a reality.

1 Introduction

Negotiation—The process through which an elegant win/win solution is reached which meets the differing needs of the two or more parties involved.

Negotiation—Part of our everyday lives

This book is for those of you who are working in companies and organisations where negotiating already forms part of your job or where it is likely to do so. It is a simple and straightforward book designed to give you information and confidence to negotiate in a variety of situations both at work and at home. Many of the skills involved are those we use in our everyday lives. In developing negotiating skills, those of living are also developed such as listening, questioning and knowing what you want.

This book assumes that you have little or no information or experience of negotiating. It will start from first principles by clarifying what it is that you want from the negotiation and providing a structure which will enable you to reach a satisfactory outcome. There is nothing 'tricksy' in this book. It will not advocate or promote smart tactics for beating the opposition.

It is designed to be light, fun and enabling so that by the time you have finished you will have more information, understanding and confidence to negotiate within and outside of your organisation. Within most chapters there are activities to help you develop your negotiating strategies and skills. The chapters are also for dipping into, with sections that are relevant to the stage that you are at.

■ *The battleground*

Negotiation has had a 'bad press'. Many publicly recorded negotiations resemble battlegrounds where there are winners and losers, often management versus the unions. Whilst the ground can be combative and difficult, the approach I use in this book assumes that there is one solution which will meet the needs of all the parties involved. Although the outcome may not be exactly the one that each party wants, respect for the other party is retained throughout and it is the arguments that are challenged.

■ *Negotiating at work*

You are probably reading this because you are already negotiating in your work and want to be more successful at it. It may be, for instance, that you remember the contract you lost with the supplier who was unable to meet your delivery time requirements. Or the appraisal interview where you accepted a pay rise less than the amount you wanted. If you think you do not already negotiate, consider the following:

- when holidays are taken in the department;
- where the office party is held;
- how to get the transfer into sales;
- negotiating the day release for the MBA;
- organising a lift to work;
- getting a day off to look after your child;
- improving your working environment.

Negotiating forms an increasing part of all our work and you may want information and ideas on how to do it well. This book will help you to become more effective.

■ *Negotiating at home*

Negotiating does not only happen at work. Many negotiations take place at home with our families and friends which may not immediately appear to be negotiation situations. For example:

- who looks after the children;
- where to take the annual summer holiday;
- who makes the beds;
- where to go on your evening out;
- who does the shopping;
- how to spend Christmas.

Christmas is a good illustration of a time we could use negotiating strategies and tactics to good effect, since at Christmas we must make a decision about how we best want to spend the festive season, with whom and where. In the many workshops I have run on negotiating, it is rare to find anyone who has spent Christmas in exactly the way they wanted. Often the decision is made out of a sense of guilt or duty, by not, for example, wanting to upset parents or in-laws.

Negotiating can be the privilege of all ages. Recently I was out shopping with my then four-year-old daughter and mentioned that I needed to go into a particular shop before going home.

She stopped me in my tracks and turning to look at me straight in the eye said, 'If you want me to go into the music shop, we'll have to go into the magazine shop first.' It was a marvellous illustration of negotiating strategy.'If I do this, will you do that?'

■■■■■■ General principles

Several key aspects that have emerged during my workshops on negotiating have become general principles for working, which I will include in the ensuing chapters. I give a brief summary here to give the flavour of some of the issues involved.

■ System and strategy

There is a system and strategy to negotiating. Logically, some aspects need to be done before others, such as being clear about what is wanted from the negotiation and how much movement is possible. This is essential before, for example, making the telephone call to arrange a meeting about a pay rise with your boss or writing the letter to the supplier renewing the contract.

This book contains a section on the strategy of negotiation, which will form a system for you to work through in any negotiations you take part in.

■ Self-confidence

I am constantly uplifted by how effective and well equipped we already are to carry out negotiations on our own behalf or on behalf of the companies we work for. What often gets in the way is a low sense of self-esteem, which results in the feeling that we are not able to negotiate. Time and time again I have seen women and men on workshops carrying out superb practice negotiations when a few hours before they were showing all the signs of a real lack of confidence.

With this in mind, this book focuses on how to develop and maintain confidence.

■ Challenge and respect

When problems arise between individuals, groups, families, companies or countries they can often be resolved by using some straightforward and well-known techniques. These include communicating, listening and being respectful, even though we may vehemently disagree with the other person's arguments.

In the model of negotiation I use, arguments can be challenged and criticised. Remember, however, that the argument isn't the person. They are doing their very best, as are you. Rather than demolish their sense of self-esteem, challenge the argument they are putting forward whilst showing your respect for them as a person.

■ *Give up blaming*

Let's give up blaming! Both ourselves and others. We need not give ourselves a hard time for the deals we have lost, the smaller pay rise we accepted, or the way we got out of the Saturday-morning supermarket shopping so that we could get to the rugby international on time.

We usually blame when we feel unable to influence a situation or a person in the hope that by doing so we will feel better about ourselves, and hence more powerful. In fact the reverse is true. Blaming undermines our sense of power and influence. If we give up blaming ourselves we are more likely to be able to change something for the better.

Think of the last time you blamed. It may have been this morning whilst you were waiting on the platform for another late train into work. It may have been the state of the office when you walked in and saw the untidy desks or wastepaper bins that had not been emptied. If you gave up blaming, what action would need to be taken?

In a much wider context, when a national problem is reported, such as the effects of bad weather disrupting travel, the first headline in the newspaper tabloids is often 'Who's to blame?' It almost seems that blaming others will make us feel better about ourselves. The situation is sometimes so awful that we can't really contemplate being responsible in any way. The reality is that we are all responsible.

So blaming does not empower ourselves or others. This book aims to increase our sense of personal influence, so with that in mind I invite you from here on to give up blaming and to assume that in every situation you *can* have influence.

■ *Negotiation means movement*

Negotiation means both parties being clear about what is ideally wanted and being prepared to move from the original position in order to reach a workable compromise. Movement is essential in negotiation, for without the commitment to move, negotiation cannot take place. This leads us to an an important distinction between influencing and negotiation:

- Influencing is a one-way process

- Negotiating is a two-way process

Influencing skills are often used in a negotiation. However, if the situation is resolved purely through persuasion, influence or logical argument then it is not negotiation. There has to be movement on both sides for a true negotiation to take place.

■ *Everybody wins*

Much of what we hear about negotiation in the press or on the television gives the impression that it is a process which is combative, where blame is apportioned to either or both sides, and where one party comes out as the 'winner' and the other as the 'loser'. This is not an image that attracts many people—it depicts negotiation as a gladiator's ring rather than a place where effective solutions can be worked out.

My aim is for all the parties involved to leave with their self-respect at least intact, if not enhanced. Negotiation is not about winning at the expense of the other person; negotiation is about each party winning, even though one side may have lost the contract to a competitor. There should be a feeling that the process has been enjoyable, energising and respectful, and that the business relationship will continue so that there will be other opportunities for negotiation in the future. By a combination of clarity of objectives, mutual respect and movement amongst many other processes, negotiation can be an enjoyable and valuable tool with which to reach a solution that satisfies everyone.

■ *Brighter and smarter*

I am often reminded that we are infinitely brighter and smarter than we give ourselves and others credit for. In this book I make some assumptions about people. For example, I think that we all have a great capacity to think clearly and that we make excellent decisions in our work and our home lives when we trust our intuition and think in a climate where we will not be criticised.

Here I work on the assumption that you are smart and bright and able to work out the best solutions to the negotiations in which you are involved. If this seems at odds with the way you think of yourself (and may be why you are reading this book in the first place) I invite you to work on the assumption that you are bright and smart throughout this book and see what happens!

Individual standpoint

You will be the person negotiating. It may well be that at times you negotiate as part of a team within your department or as part of your circle of friends or family and for you I do include a chapter on team negotiation. Essentially, this book is written from an individual standpoint and the examples assume a face-to-face negotiation between yourself and another person.

World leaders negotiate issues involving people and countries with implications that can be far-reaching and formidable. In its ultimate context the ability to negotiate can save lives and prevent wars. Although it is more likely that your negotiations will have much smaller implications, they are equally important: they affect you personally, or may have repercussions within your work.

I hope you too will find negotiating an enjoyable and exciting search for the one solution that suits us all.

Good luck!

Activity Sheet 1

Successful outcomes

Think of a time when a situation was resolved well. It could be one you observed or one in which you took part.

■ Describe what happened.

■ What specifically contributed to the successful outcome?

2 Setting Objectives

Is this where I was going?

I have not seen the plays in town
only the computer printouts
I have not read the latest books
only 'The Wall Street Journal'
I have not heard birds sing this year
only the ringing of phones
I have not taken a walk anywhere
but from the parking lot to my office
I have not shared a feeling in years
but my thoughts are known to all
I have not listened to my own needs
but what I want I get
I have not shed a tear in ages
I have arrived
Is this where I was going?

Natasha Josefowitz (Warner, 1983)

Natasha Josefowitz's poem poignantly indicates how we can go through life doing what we think we want without really questioning where it is that we really want to be and what we really want to be doing. In negotiating, as in life, it is a crucial first step to be clear of where we want to be, or what outcome we want from the negotiation. As the saying goes:

'If you don't know where you're going, you'll probably end up somewhere else.'

(Campbell, 1974)

◼ Is it negotiable?

This chapter will help you identify a situation that you want to
negotiate and to assess whether the situation is negotiable at all. It
may be, for example, that you want to negotiate a pay rise in return
for transferring to a new department and taking on new
responsibilities, including supervision or management of others.
The company may be in recession, with redundancies imminent, so
the likelihood of promotion now is unrealistic. The situation you
want to negotiate may well not be feasible and will need
reassessment. I mentioned in the introduction that a situation can be
resolved by powerful argument or influence and this can be an
effective and appropriate strategy. *But remember that unless there is
a possibility of movement by both parties the situation is not a
negotiable one.*

◼ *Am I the best person?*

This chapter will also help you clarify whether you are the best
person to negotiate. By this I mean that although the situation may
be negotiable, you are not in the best position to negotiate it. For
example, a contract with a key client may need renewing, and
although this falls into your area of work you know that you are on
the move from the department and your successor will be coming in
a couple of weeks' time. In this case it is more appropriate for you
to work with the new incumbent and assist him/her to manage the
negotiation. This in itself can be valuable in terms of training
someone else in negotiation and providing them with an entry into
the work of the department.

It is completely acceptable to recognise that you are not at this
moment in a position to negotiate well. This may be, for example,
because of lack of information or power to influence. As Marketing
Executive, for example, you may not have sufficient organisational
weight to negotiate with the other party, so it may be better to hand
this over to another person. Whilst it may seem like a failure, in fact
there is power in saying: 'No, I recognise that Mr Brown is better

equipped to negotiate this situation.'

■ *Is this the best time?*

A more personal example. It may be that you want to renegotiate with your partner where you take this year's holiday. You have an important project at work which is going to last at least another three weeks and your attention will be fully stretched for this period and maybe longer. Where you spend your holiday is negotiable, but this may not be the very best time to do it. It is always possible simply to tell your partner that you want to talk about it and set up a time to do that. In the mean time maybe have some initial discussions over a meal.

Always ask yourself the question: 'Is this the best time?' Often the reality is that at work or home we cannot always make the decisions we want at the time we want, so having asked yourself the question and recognised that this isn't the best time, you may find that you have to do it anyway.

■ *Doing it anyway*

The important point at this stage is to acknowledge that this isn't the best time to negotiate. Take this into account when assessing your influence and strength in the situation. If this is a pressing negotiation which falls into your job role, other parts of your workload may have to take lower priority and you will need to have more help or information in order to take this negotiation on. Think of a time when you want to negotiate and ask yourself:

- Is this situation negotiable?
- Am I the best person to negotiate?
- Is this the time to do it?

So far, so good. The next step is to think about the situation in more detail and imagine the ideal outcome.

Identifying clearly what it is we really want from the negotiation and keeping this in mind makes the whole process much more straightforward and logical.

Think your biggest picture

Visualising is an important strategy for anticipating all possible outcomes. From this biggest picture realistic steps and goals can be extracted, to help achieve the negotiated settlement. It is from this biggest picture that our creativity comes. When faced with a problem we think of one or two possible solutions, depending on our previous experience and how much ability we have to think laterally.

This is called 'convergent thinking': it resembles having tunnel vision, from a problem to a solution.

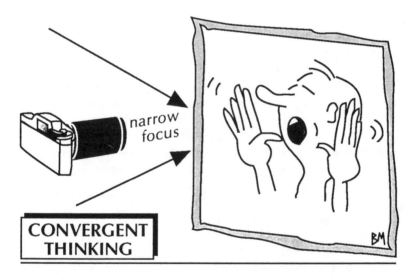

narrow focus

CONVERGENT THINKING

An alternative is to think of all the possible solutions to a problem. This is called 'divergent thinking'.

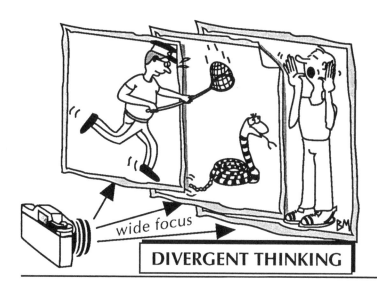

wide focus

DIVERGENT THINKING

▆▆▆▆ What do you really want?

If we have a clear idea of what we *really* want, this can make the difference between possibly achieving and really getting what we want. For those who find visualising easy, the question to ask now is: *What do I really want from this negotiation?*

> *In the negotiation workshops I run, each participant thinks about and plans for a negotiation, which they carry out with another member of the course. They have time to plan, to focus on all the elements of strategy we are covering here, and they have an opportunity to practise the skills of negotiating which we shall be covering later.*
>
> *After they have taken part in the role play I ask them to clarify once again what they were setting out to do. Despite the information, the opportunities to think and plan, they are often still unclear about what they were aiming to achieve, so it is no surprise to them that the negotiation itself didn't proceed as planned.*

So consider the question: 'What do I really want?' Allow thoughts or images to come into your mind, for the first thoughts to a question are often the most accurate. For example, if I ask you how you would *really* like to spend next Christmas, what is your immediate response? Allow your first thoughts and reactions to enter your head. The important point here is that although you may not necessarily act on these thoughts, visualising the ideas is a way of making choices about the future.

Whatever images or thoughts have come to mind in response to this question, write them down or represent them on paper in whatever way suits you best. This is your own time and your own thoughts so logical thinking or clarity of expression is of no importance. If you find you can represent your thoughts more easily by drawings, sketches or doodles, put those down. A picture is a much more powerful image than words.

■ *Take time out*

For the many of us who find visualising an ideal outcome a challenge, try the following:

Take at least five minutes out of your day. If this in itself is difficult make an appointment with yourself in your diary. You make appointments with others and give them your time, so why not yourself? If necessary and to save any embarrassment with your colleagues give yourself a fictitious client name.

To ensure that you are not interrupted for those five minutes choose a quiet place where you will not be observed. If this isn't possible, take time out on the train or bus travelling to work, or stop the car for five minutes on your way home. Walk the dog, sit in your favourite chair in the evening or play a sport. I have found that some of my best ideas have come whilst swimming lengths of the pool. Take the time whenever it most suits you and where there is a safe place for you to be able to think clearly.

■■■■■■ Change means upheaval

If you are unused to negotiating and to taking the time to imagine your ideal outcome, this activity may seem strange. It is worth remembering that change always means upheaval. Recognise that there is no more time available. Time is not infinite. In order to make the time to do something new, such as visualisation, you may have to let go of something else.

Taking part in these activities will feel awkward at the beginning and possibly embarrassing. Expect this and welcome it, treating it lightly and easily. The situation is important but not serious!

Now with your five minutes:

Allow your body to get into the most comfortable position. Uncross your feet or legs, allow your hands to rest on your lap and, starting with your feet, take two or three minutes to relax your body by focusing your attention first on your toes, your feet, your ankles and your legs. Gradually work your way up your body. Pay particular attention to your neck and shoulders and as you think of each part, allow that part of your body to relax so that there is no muscular tension. By the end of this activity your body should be sufficiently relaxed to allow your mind to wander. As it wanders think about the end of the negotiation and where you want to be.

- What does it look like?

- What has happened?

- What has been achieved?

- What is the atmosphere like between you?

Allow your thoughts to include everything that enters your head. Do not judge or select at this stage, but imagine yourself in that end situation. Let us assume that you are negotiating for a contract with a new client. If the negotiation goes exactly as you want:

- What will it look like?
- How much money will be involved?
- What will the order be?
- What will your position be like in the company?
- What will your standing be with the client and the client's company?

Again, think your biggest picture and allow your mind to wander. At the end of the five minutes take a piece of paper and write down all the thoughts and images that come to mind about your ideal outcome. This will form the basis of your negotiation; in the subsequent chapters we will revise and hone your image so that it becomes a workable strategy. Hold on to your dreams.

Movement

Having clarified what it is you want the next step is to plan a series of positions within which you can negotiate. It is important here to have a range of options so that movement can be made and an outcome reached that suits both parties. In general, the greater the range of movement, the more readily a negotiated settlement will be reached. As mentioned in the introduction, if movement is not possible from one or both sides then other strategies will need to be used, such as influencing or persuasion.

Essentially, in any negotiation, there are three key positions to be identified. In setting your objectives, being clear and concise about these positions will go a long way towards success.

The three key positions

Ideal outcome

If the situation were ideally resolved, how would it be? You will have already spent some time clarifying and realising this ideal position in the earlier part of this chapter.

■ *Realistic outcome*

What would be a realistic, as opposed to an ideal outcome? This may be based on previous experience, such as the percentage pay rise you've achieved in previous appraisal interviews. So whilst ideally you may want an 11 per cent pay increase, in the light of current practice and current wage negotiations, 7 to 8 per cent may be more likely.

■ *Fallback position*

In all negotiations it is important to clarify for yourself the minimum standard or position that you will accept. For example, you may want to move from your current area of work into a new department. Ideally you want to move within six months. Yet you know that with the organisational changes going on and the training you need to take up the new position, ten to eleven months is a more realistic prediction. However, your baseline may be that if you are not in the new department in fifteen months' time you are going to look for another job.

Whatever the range within these three positions, it is important to know what it is, so that in the negotiation you know to what extent you are prepared to move.

Summary

This chapter has focused on:

- the best time;
- the best person;
- whether this is negotiable;
- identifying and anchoring the biggest picture;
- the settlement that is wanted.

Having answered the basic questions you are now in a position to move forward. If the situation is not negotiable, or this is not the time to do it, you will need to place it on the back burner to await or plan for a time that is more appropriate. The next chapter addresses more specifically your individual role and influence within the negotiation. In other words, your power to negotiate.

Activity Sheet 2

Think of a situation you want to negotiate. Briefly describe it, including the scenario and the people who are involved.

■ Is this situation negotiable? (Can there be movement on both sides?)

■ Am I the best person to negotiate?

■ Is this the best time?

■ What do I want from the negotiation?

3 Power

You are a lot more powerful than you think you are, and others aren't nearly as weak.

Self-esteem and confidence are the cornerstone of effective negotiation.

Rosabeth Moss Kanter is Professor of Business Administration at Harvard Business School and one of the leading exponents of management thinking in the world today. In her book, *Men and Women of the Corporation,* she defines power in an organisation as: 'The ability to mobilise resources outside of one's unit as well as within it,' and continues: 'The powerful are the ones who have access to the tools for action.'

Being powerful means being able to make things happen. In negotiating it embraces all that we have covered so far in terms of being clear about the objective, recognising your own ability in the situation and determining what needs to be done to reach the outcome.

Having identified what it is that you want from the negotiation, you are likely to be in one of two positions:

- Recognising that the negotiation is bigger than you anticipated and that you need more power and influence;

- Recognising that you have more power and influence than you anticipated.

Whatever the position, this chapter will help you to analyse how much power you have, how much power the other party has and how to develop your confidence to negotiate. These elements will form a basis for the next step, which is the detailed positions of the negotiation.

▰▰▰▰ Types of power

French and Raven, in *The Bases of Social Power,* identified six types of power found in organisations. As you read through the different definitions, make a note of the type of power you have in the negotiation.

1. Reward power

This is the ability to deliver positive consequences or remove negative ones. For example, a manager who can recommend a person for promotion, or a supplier who can offer an extra 5 per cent discount, is exercising reward power. A manager who helps one of his or her staff, by dealing with the results of an order going astray is exercising reward power by removing the negative consequences. Similarly, a manager who separates two staff who are working ineffectively on a project because of interpersonal difficulties, is exercising reward power.

2. Coercive power

This is the ability to remove positive consequences or to deliver negative ones. For example, a parent saying to his or her children, 'If you don't clear up your bedroom, we won't go skateboarding today', is exercising coercive power. Similarly a person making a promotion or demotion on the basis of race or gender discrimination is exercising coercive power.

3. Information power

Here a person is seen as having information central to others achieving their goal. This information is not available elsewhere. The tea-person in an organisation is frequently a source of this type of power, though is rarely seen as such. (She or he can also use coercive power: for example delivering strong tea or no iced buns on Thursday.) Strategic planners and accountants are often seen as possessing information power for they have access to information about the company and the direction in which it is going.

4. Referent power

This is much more personally based. Others identify with someone who has referent power, or want to be like them. It may be that this person possesses a particular trait, such as charisma, eloquence or popularity. Here the power is in the person themselves and what s/he can get others to do.

5. Expert power

People are perceived as having some special knowledge or skill, for example in information technology or graphic design; or the ability to come up with creative solutions to problems.

6. Legitimate or role power

The power that comes with the job. The position a person holds gives them influence over issues and people because of their special role or responsibilities.

Most people have a combination of the above types of power. Paint as broad a picture as you can of all the information, ideas and expertise that you bring to the negotiation. As mentioned before in deciding what you want from this negotiation, you can also represent power on a piece of paper in the way that suits you best. It may be using words, phrases, diagrams or pictures. Do not be restrained by any rules but simply put down your thoughts in whatever way seems appropriate to you.

For example:
- knowledge about your job, both technical and social;
- communication skills;
- commitment to resolving the problem;
- the relationship you have with the other party;
- your experience of your area of work gained both in your current company and perhaps in others;
- your ideas;
- a sense of humour;
- knowledge about the other party's organisation.

Now consider the situation from the other party's point of view. What power do they have? For example:

- They may have information which you do not have.
- They may have competitors bidding against you for the same deal.
- They may be deliberately withholding information.
- Are they putting their best operator, in a more senior position than you are, into the deal?

Again paint the broadest picture possible and represent it in picture, words or doodles.
- How does the power balance look?
- Where are there similarities between you?
- Where are there differences?
- What are you going to do about them?

Write down your immediate thoughts.

By now you should have an idea of the different types of power that you bring into the negotiation, the power of the other party and where the balance of power lies.

◼ Perception of power

It is the perception of power which affects the behaviour of others rather than their actual resources. This may seem to contradict what has just been said, but both are true. It is important to know the different types of power that exist in organisations as well as recognising that perceptions can vary as to the power we assume others have. I'm sure you will recognise the following examples:

- The computer buff, who knows every aspect of software and hardware currently on the market and is a fund of information. He or she may have little role power, yet is seen as possessing considerable information or expert power.

- The person who issues the wages or who reimburses travelling expenses exercises reward power or, some would say, coercive power. Again they can be seen as very powerful even though the role power may be quite low.

Power is often seen as a limited quantity. If one person has it, another can't have it. By this definition, power in a negotiation is seen as something to exercise over others which will tip the scales in favour of one party over the other. This is where the concept of negotiation becomes win/lose rather than win/win.

Rosabeth Moss Kanter defines power to include autonomy rather than aggression or dominance. That is, all parties in a negotiation have a right to be considered intelligent and treated respectfully, to express what they want from a negotiation, and to be listened to.

At the end of this chapter are two activities. The first is designed to remind you of what it is like to feel good about yourself and hence more powerful. Both activities provide a range of things for you to do at a time of your own choice. Using these questions you can begin to build into your daily life some of the activities that make you feel good about yourself, to increase your sense of self-confidence and self-esteem in negotiating. Start small, with a short or small activity that can be easily achieved today, for example, walking via the park to the railway station, stopping off at the library, phoning that friend you haven't seen for a long while and fixing a lunch date.

Try to do one of these activities each day. If that seems too ambitious a task, aim to do one a week and gradually increase it to two a week, and so on. Good luck!

The second activity will enable you to assess the nature of your own power and that of the other party. Having upgraded and uplifted your sense of power and identified that of the other party, the next chapter will return to strategy. It will look at the movement needed to negotiate effectively and the specific objectives to aim for in negotiating.

Activity Sheet 3

Write down all your first thoughts.

■ Write down all the activities that you most enjoy doing. Yes, all of them. Periodically return to this question and keep adding to the list.

■ How does carrying out these activities make you feel?

■ What is one activity on your list that you can do today?

Activity Sheet 4

■ Think of a situation that you want to negotiate in and briefly describe it.

■ What is it that you want? (Refer to Chapter 2.)

■ What different types of power do you have? (Refer to the six types of power in this chapter.)

■ Now consider the other party's power. Using the same definitions, what power do they have?

■ Where is there a balance of power? What power do they have that you don't?

■ In the light of your answer to the above, what needs to change for the power to be more evenly distributed ?

4 Planning Your Strategy

We have more in common than differences.

Beneath the surface

In many ways the process of negotiation resembles an iceberg: the
actual negotiation that takes place is the tip that is visible above the
surface. That discussion is the result of many hours, days, even
weeks or months, of planning and preparation.

Another analogy is a manufacturing plant: the salespeople will have
a daunting, if not impossible task to sell a product that has not been
refined and developed by the production department, and they in
turn are affected by any changes that research and development
produce. In any system there is a synthesis and integration of parts
to form the whole, and negotiation is similar to this. For example, an
appraisal interview is not simply the discussion that takes place
between a manager and his or her subordinate about the work done
over the previous year and plans for the next twelve months. If both
sides haven't thought about what is wanted over the next year, much
of the discussion will be fruitless. Inherent in negotiation is a huge
amount of planning, thinking and consideration of alternative ideas.

Planning

So here we are still in the submerged part of the iceberg, thinking
and planning for the negotiation itself. The 90 per cent of the
iceberg that is present below the surface is essential to keeping the
pinnacle of the iceberg afloat.

■ *What is known?*

As well as identifying the movement that can be made within the
negotiation it is important also to consider what the other party
wants from the negotiation. We need to make some projections and
estimations based on what we actually know and what we have to
assume. The information may be known to us because of previous
contact. But if this is a new client, finding out this information
through other sources and through listening well to the client's
responses, both verbal and written, plays a key part at this stage.

■ *Overlap*

The follow-on from this estimation results in identifying where, if at
all, there is an overlap between your expectations and those of the
other party. Is there an overlap, for example, on the price per
product that you will pay? Is there an overlap on the fact that each
of you wants to continue to do business with the other? The
continuation of the relationship may be part of the common ground.
The next step is identifying those three key positions mentioned in
chapter 2:

- Your ideal settlement (IS). This means identifying
  ideally what it is you want from the negotiation. You
  have probably already clarified this when you set your
  objectives (Chapter 2).

- Realistic settlement (RS). What is realistically
  attainable? This is different from the ideal and is based
  on past practice, past experience and the information
  available.

- Fallback position (FBP). This is the minimum standard
  or condition acceptable.

Negotiating means being able to move from your original objective
and being able to operate within a range of options. Take the
example of negotiating a pay rise.

You

Ideal settlement (IS)
Your ideal settlement is a 10 per cent pay increase to cover imbalances from the previous two years, new responsibilities you have taken on, inflation and so on.

Realistic settlement (RS)
The current round of wage negotiations is settling at around 7.5 per cent

Fallback position (FBP).
The minimum increase acceptable is 7 per cent, below which you will be looking in the newspaper columns for other jobs. On a scale it would look like this:

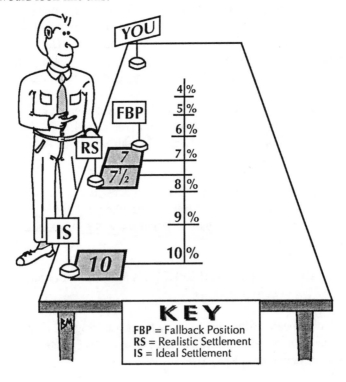

KEY
FBP = Fallback Position
RS = Realistic Settlement
IS = Ideal Settlement

The Manager

Ideal settlement (IS) is 6 per cent. The recession, inflation, potential redundancies, market share, and so on all affect the amount that can be offered.

Realistically (RS) 7 per cent is around the figure that current settlements are reaching.

Fallback position (FBP): the highest rate possible would be 8.5 per cent without major ramifications throughout the company.

KEY
FBP = Fallback Position
RS = Realistic Settlement
IS = Ideal Settlement

If we combine these two diagrams we end up with the following:

In this example there is an overlap, between 7 per cent and 8.5 per cent, within which the two parties can negotiate. So the pay rise can settle within these two figures. As a general principle, the wider the range, the greater the opportunity for negotiation. Here there is a 1.5

per cent overlap, which in wage negotiations can provide quite a wide and flexible bargaining range.

■ Common ground

There has to be common ground between the parties involved. Other examples of common ground are:

- commitment to doing business together;
- good working relationship;
- goodwill;
- wanting both parties to profit from the negotiation;
- commitment to resolving the issue/problem;
- the benefit to another party that this negotiation will provide.

It is important to identify this common ground with the other party. It is difficult to anticipate what the other party wants from the negotiation and how much movement they are prepared to make. So central to the planning of the negotiation are:

- considering and anticipating the range of options;
- good listening during the negotiation itself;
- establishing where the overlaps are.

Take another example of negotiating Christmas.

> *For many this begins about mid-October when the first suggestions start to be piled on the table. You have had your family each Christmas for a number of years and would like to try to find some alternatives to the usual four-day stay. You have already hinted about visiting friends and wanting some time for yourself.*

You

Ideal

You want your family to come for Christmas Day itself.

Realistic

Because of the distance involved, travelling on the 24th is more appropriate, and staying overnight until Boxing Day.

Fallback position

The family arrive on the 24th December and stay until the 27th.

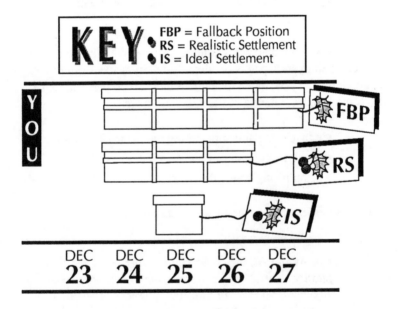

What do you think the family's expectations might be?

Family

Ideal
The ideal is to arrive on the 23rd and stay until the 27th. Travelling would be easier and there would be more time for a proper family break.

Realistic
To travel on the 24th and stay over until the 26th. The family know that you are visiting friends for the New Year and want to go to the sales before then.

Fallback position
The least favoured option would be to travel on Christmas Day itself but to stay over at least until Boxing Day.

On a diagram the three positions would look like this:

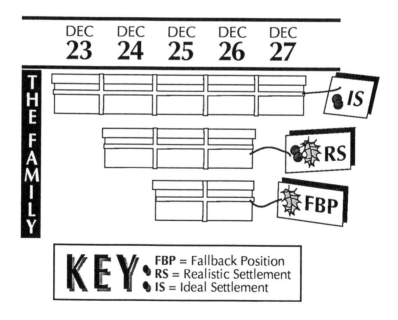

These two situations placed together produce the following:

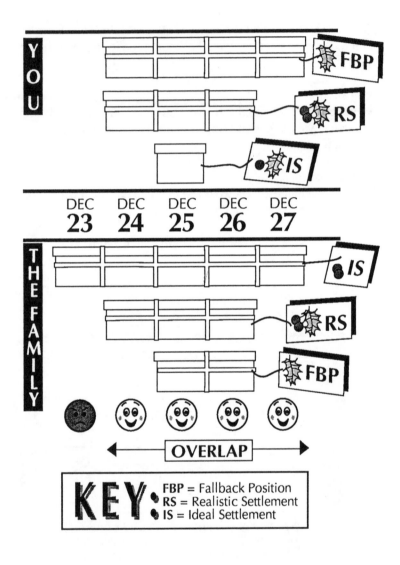

Here there is an overlap of interest between the 24th and 27th of December, with both of you having a similar realistic settlement (RS). So the arrangement for Christmas is likely to be one of the following:

- The family arrive on the 25th and stay until the 26th.
- They arrive on the 24th and stay until the 26th.
- They arrive on the 24th and stay until the 27th.

Rarely, however, are negotiations as straightforward as this example, which involves just one element, i.e. dates. Usually there are other criteria which impact or can be included in the negotiation. In this example of Christmas these are:

- how often the family are together during the year;
- who else is able to have the family for Christmas;
- what else you would rather be doing at Christmas.

This introduces another key notion in negotiating.

■ Trade-offs

Trade-offs are elements that you are prepared to concede in order to reach the outcome you want. This might mean having the family for Christmas from the 23rd to 27th of December this year on the understanding that next Christmas you will go skiing with friends.

So a key phrase here is: *'If...then...'*.

The concept of giving or conceding an issue in order to gain in the negotiation or conclude it is a key distinction between influencing and negotiating. Conceding means movement means negotiating. For example: 'We'd be delighted for you to come on the 23rd December and stay until the 27th this year. If that happens, how would it be if we spend next year abroad or with friends, as we've been thinking of doing for some time?'

■ *Don't give without getting!*

Concede in order to get something in return. For example:

- If I increase the order by another 500 units, will you give me an extra 5 per cent discount?
- If I do the washing up will you make the beds?

My daughter and I have different objectives at bedtime. She wants to stay up for as long as possible; I want her to go to bed as soon as possible. I have considerable power as an adult and as a parent, whereas hers lies in personal influence, ability to shout and deliver negative consequences such as simply saying: 'No.'

It was nearly bedtime and my daughter was pushing for more time to finish the game she was playing. 'Another ten minutes,' she said.
'Five,' I said.
'Ten.'
'Five,' I said again.
'No!'
'OK. How about this? If you have another ten minutes finishing your game, we'll have one story in bed rather than two.'
'OK,' she said.
'Deal?'
'Deal.'

The pull is to give something up, for example to lower the price or to accept a longer delivery time, particularly when the negotiation is getting tough or conflict is emerging. This is one of the most frequent tendencies I have come across in workshops. The answer to the pressure to give something up in the face of adversity or conflict is... don't! Only give something away in order to get something back that you want:

- 'I will accept a 6.5 per cent pay increase now and continue to supervise the new project, which will prevent you having to recruit somebody new into the job, if in five months' time my pay is increased by a further 2 per cent to give a total of 8.5 per cent.'

- 'If you help me tidy up the toys we can get to the park in half an hour.'

- 'I'll accept early retirement if I can work fifty days on contract during the following two years.'

Summary

Planning your strategy means:

- building on clear objectives;
- having a realistic assessment of your power;
- having a realistic assessment of the power of the other party;
- identifying the three positions within which you are prepared to move;
- being prepared to move from your original position;
- identifying common ground;
- using phrases such as 'if...then'.

This concludes the preparation in terms of strategy. In the next chapter we shall look at preparation for the negotiation.

Activity Sheet 5

■ Identify a situation to negotiate. Briefly describe it.

■ Objective. What do you want out of the negotiation? Be as specific as you can.

■ Power. How much power do you have? Be as wide as possible in your analysis.

■ What is your ideal outcome? Again, be as specific as possible.

■ What is a realistic outcome? Consider this in detail.

■ Fallback position. What minimum standard or criteria will you accept?

Activity Sheet 6

Now look at the negotiation from the other party's point of view.

■ Objective. What do you think they want from the negotiation?

■ Power. How much power and influence does the other party have and in what way is it different from the power that you have ?

■ What do you think is their:

  (a) ideal settlement?

  (b) realistic settlement?

  (c) fallback postion?

■ What common ground is there between you? If little or none exists reconsider your original objective.

■ On what issues are you prepared to negotiate, i.e. what concessions will you make?

5 Preparing for the Negotiation

It ain't what you do, it's the way that you do it. That's what gets results.
(From the song by Sy Oliver & James Young © 1939
Leeds Music Corp./MCA Music Ltd.)

By now you should be clear about where you are heading and what you are prepared to negotiate with—that is, the concessions you will make. The next step is to move towards the tip of the iceberg and conduct a negotiation itself. This chapter includes further elements of planning: where to conduct the negotiation, how best to practise, the best time to negotiate, and who can help. In addition, if you are feeling excited, anxious, even scared, this chapter will help you manage some of the feelings involved. Keep in mind a negotiation of your own choice so that the following can be applied directly to it.

In preparation for the negotiation, let's set the scene under four main headings:

When Where What Who

When

When is the best time to negotiate:

- for you?

- for the other party?

Think about the best time in the day for you to negotiate. Some of us are morning people—that is we have most energy in the first half of the day; others come into their own in the twilight hours. Identify your optimum time.

What about the other party? When do you think would be their optimum time? For example, if you are negotiating with a client who frequently has business lunches, negotiating at three o'clock after a heavy lunch may well do neither of you much justice. Arrange for a morning meeting or call on a day when both of you are relatively free from other pressures.

The length of time available to negotiate is important too. Buying and selling a house is one of the most stressful activities that both vendors and buyers undergo and much of the negotiations and arrangements is done in almost a minus time frame. Decisions have to be made quickly and immediately because of competition with other purchasers. So whilst you might, for instance, consider increasing your offer as a house buyer, the decision may need to be a fast one. In this situation, reconsider your original objective. How much do you want the property? If your answer is 'greatly', what is the price of haggling over a few hundred or even a few thousand pounds, if the property is really what you want?

I will say more later about the best timing for specific types of negotiation, but included in this is the ability to say 'no' when, for example, an agent or a client is pushing you to make a decision quickly that won't be in your best interest. As with all negotiations it is a question of balance. A longer time frame may mean that you lose the deal. Not having time to think may also mean that you lose the deal or do not get the settlement that you ideally want, for if you have to think quickly often the thinking is not clear and you make decisions that you may regret later on. In summary, consider when would be the most appropriate timing to begin the negotiation. Find a balance between making sufficient time for discussions (allowing for lack of replies to deadlines etc.), and giving away so much time that the initiative is lost.

■ *Where to negotiate?*

There is much discussion in organisations about the space that a person has, and frequently it is linked to status or hierarchy. For example the type of office furniture or size of carpet is often an indicator of someone's position in the organisation, and power is frequently given over to that stamp of authority.

■ *Territory*

Individually we have a territory, or a space around us, and we can feel uncomfortable if people encroach upon this. Notice the reactions of people who are cramped together in a lift. Rarely do conversations take place unless those involved know one another. Eyes are often averted and attention focused on the next floor the lift will stop at or the different types of shoes people are wearing. We have a boundary around us which differs between individuals and between cultures. For example, in Mediterranean countries it is much more appropriate and comfortable for individuals to stand physically close together to greet one another, which they do much more warmly than in Britain. Men rarely just shake hands with other men; usually they embrace one another.

This type of behaviour is frequently seen as embarrassing to men in other cultures. Many UK organisations traditionally prefer to keep people at a distance and shake hands more formally. Whatever your boundary, the main point is to recognise it and acknowledge and also recognise the boundary of the other person. They may prefer to be formal whereas you find it easy to greet in a more friendly and open way. Again it is finding the balance that will make both of you feel at ease and prepared to move the negotiation on.

The issue of territory also relates to where you meet to negotiate. There is comfort and power in meeting on your own home ground, and that is also likely to be the case for the other party. As meeting in their office or on their premises may undermine your sense of self-confidence, consider where would be the best place for both of you. What about a neutral ground such as a quiet restaurant or a club if you have one?

■ *Think creatively*

If you and the other party are separated by some distance look at the geography of the area half-way between you. Is there an uplifting place for you to meet? A historic building or a place of natural beauty where there is likely to be a quiet spot for you to discuss your business? Contact the local tourist information bureau and find out about other good meeting places.

A more creative and enjoyable location is likely to register far more in the other person's mind and contribute to your effectiveness and influence as a negotiator, than meeting on your home base in an open-plan office where you are likely to be interrupted and affected by other people's conversations and telephone calls.

■ *Aim for the best*

What you are entering into is important for each of you and deserves enjoyable and uplifting surroundings. Consider what else is likely to be going on at the date and time of your meeting.

> *When I married, the church we chose was very near to a river resort popular with sailors and rowing enthusiasts. Little did I know that the Saturday we had chosen coincided with the annual rowing regatta and with a lull in the races during the afternoon, instead of an expected handful waiting outside the church, there were upwards of several hundred.*
>
> *In the event it added to the excitement and enjoyment of the day, though had I been wanting a relatively small, quiet affair, I would have been greatly disappointed.*

■ *What tools to use*

Consider the best means of negotiating:

- for yourself;
- for the other person.

What might be appropriate for you may well not suit the other party. Let us assume you are negotiating the contract for a new work with an author's agent. The agent is experienced, confident, has other publishers interested in the work, and is frequently condescending in approach. Their preference may be for spontaneous and frequently inconvenient telephone conversations with you when you are in the middle of something else and cannot think clearly enough to respond efficiently.

Your preference may be different: an initial letter identifying the purpose of the contact, an indication of what you are aiming for. Some boundaries ending with a commitment to call on a certain day to talk about it may give you more confidence and preparation time.

While most of this book is about one-to-one negotiations with another person, within that area there are many permutations. We communicate:

- in person;
- by letter;
- on the telephone;
- by faxes and telexes.

Much communication is a combination of these methods. I have often heard arguments for phoning the other party at a time inappropriate to them, for example when they have come back from a lengthy board meeting, in order to undermine their power and make the negotiation easier for yourself. My response is easy and always the same:

- If you are aiming for a win/win situation and a negotiation that suits you both, does this action contribute towards that outcome?

- You might achieve your aim and get the deal—but at what expense?

- If you truthfully asked yourself how you felt at the end of the negotiation what would your answer be?

- Do you feel good about using that particular strategy? How do you think the other party will feel? They may have said yes in the short term, but will they come back and continue business with you?

As another illustration consider the business the other party is in. In a fast-moving business, telephoning the client may well not be the best initiative. An initial letter will alert him or her to the situation so that they will know you are following up with a telephone call and can prepare an assistant to take the call when it comes in. Aim not to throw surprises. The essence of good negotiating is for both parties to be able to think clearly and make intelligent decisions in a climate free of abuse.

■ *Who can help?*

Much of this book is designed for you to work through individually yet having an ally in the form of a partner or a work colleague— even a mirror at home, a dictaphone or the family cat—can help you practise negotiating skills, in particular how to begin the conversation, the telephone call or the meeting. In the same way that you took time out to think about what you wanted in the negotiation in Chapter 2, take time to practise the negotiation before you put pen to paper or make a call. The initial contact and the last thing that is said in a conversation are those that are remembered most clearly. What impression do you want to convey to the other party? If you are telephoning, think about your opening remark, especially if the other party does not know you and has to imagine who you are by the message that is coming down the telephone line, which will be purely auditory.

Meeting face to face is a much easier option (for some people), which we will explore in more detail in a later chapter, though for some people I know, speaking on the telephone or negotiating via letter is much more comfortable, certainly where there are great distances involved and sometimes continents.

Dealing with feelings

Negotiating for the first time or aiming to do it differently, and therefore better, is going to mean a change. However, the process of change may bring up feelings that can get in the way of taking any action. It may be that at this moment you are feeling anxious about taking the next step: making the telephone call, writing the letter, arranging the meeting with your boss about your pay rise and so on.

Sometimes these feelings can actually prevent us taking the action required, so addressing them at this stage is important. Doing something differently involves a change, and change brings upheaval. Expect that negotiating in a new way for you will mean upheaval and welcome it.

If you are now beginning to feel immobilised sneak a look at the worst scenario.

- In this negotiation, what's the worst that can happen?
- If the worst happens what will that really be like?
- What needs to happen, for this scenario not to take place?
- Who or what can help?

By now you should be in one of two places:

- Feeling less anxious, having understood that the fear you experienced has no real bearing on the reality of the negotiation: that it is perfectly possible to negotiate well in the situation you are in.

or

- The fear you have experienced is appropriate. The situation may be bigger than you imagined or you are not in the best position to negotiate at present. Whatever the reason, go back and reassess your original objective and power.

As a general guideline aim to trust your thinking and the first thoughts that you have in tackling a new situation or your immediate response to a question put to you. Recognise also that your thinking and feeling are two different aspects of yourself and trusting your feelings may not always be the best indicator of appropriate action. Wherever possible, look at the reality of the situation rather than any sense of fear or anxiety. Remember the line: 'The disaster you are expecting has already happened'.

■ *Feelings—not always the best guide to action*

Let us assume for a moment that you are not feeling totally up to this task. It may be that as a result of your analysis of the situation you need to review your power or reassess your initial goal in the negotiation, including whether you are the best person for the job. What is important is to distinguish between:

- how you feel;
- what you think;
- what is reality.

Logical analysis tells you that this situation is negotiable, that you are the right person for the job, that you can be clear about what is achievable and recognise the power that you and the other party have. Yet despite this logical overview, you may be feeling totally inadequate. It is perfectly acceptable to feel anxious before the negotiation. What is important is to recognise that acting on the feelings of fear, caution or anxiety during the negotiation is not the way to proceed successfully. Whilst you may feel unsure, or lacking in confidence, you don't have to show this uncertainty and indeed much of the time, particularly at work, you act logically and rationally even though you may be feeling quite differently.

So think about how you feel and whether this is simply a feeling that you can laugh about, have a quiet shake about, or get rid of by talking about it with a colleague. If possible, set up a talking partnership with someone you enjoy being with and trust. It could be someone at work, a friend or partner at home. Set some time aside to hear one another on whatever issue or problem is concerning each of you at the moment. Whilst one speaks, the other listens with attention riveted. The talking partner uses the listener to help clarify their thoughts. Often by talking it through you can sort out the reality of the feeling. Sometimes it is a smart indicator of what you should do next.

> *Some years ago I ran a development programme for supervisors who worked in branches of a large financial institution. One of the women had recently been promoted to train new staff in branch procedures, which was her area of work. She came to me one evening confiding her fear at the prospect of being responsible to train other people. 'I don't know anything,' she protested. 'I can't possibly do this.' She couldn't think ahead about any enjoyment or benefit she or her trainees might get.*
>
> *I suggested that she write down everything that she knew about her job, which she would be training others in. She went off to her room thoughtfully, prepared to give it a try. At breakfast the next morning I asked her how she got on. Smiling broadly she said: 'I stopped writing after four*

> *pages of foolscap. I was amazed at how much I knew.'*
>
> *She was later promoted and went on to become one of the best area trainers in the organisation.*

■ *Feeling good about yourself*

Feeling good about yourself enhances your energy, your ability to make things happen and your general sense of well-being about life and the world around you. How you see and present yourself is of key importance. Here are three questions to ask yourself before you proceed:

- What is going well for me at the moment, either at work or at home, and in particular what could contribute to the successful outcome of the negotiation?

- What is not going so well or could get in the way of negotiating effectively?

- What do I need in order to enhance my confidence in the negotiation?

■ Image

Research has shown that for women working in organisations their promotion depended on:

- 60 per cent image;
- 30 per cent exposure;
- 10 per cent ability.

Even allowing for statistical error ('There are lies, damn lies and statistics' – Mark Twain) image is clearly a crucial factor. Consider what your image is. Is it as you would wish it to be? How could it be different? In years of work with both women and men in organisations I have rarely found anyone who is genuinely at home in his or her body. Mostly we feel critical or dispirited about the way we look and would willingly change great chunks of ourselves to improve our image. Note the huge business in so-called self-improvement such as slimming aids, cosmetics, clothes and fitness centres.

The media message generally is that if you are slimmer, faster, wear certain clothes or drive a certain car, you will be successful, popular, happy and more effective in your work. However, as thousands of people will testify, changing all these elements will not necessarily change the person within.

■ *Start from where you are*

The reality is that you are as you are and acknowledging and accepting yourself for who you are and where you are now is a crucial starting point for making any changes. There is no point in wishing or pretending that you could be someone different. This is the body that you have this time around; you might as well enjoy it.

■ *Self–acceptance*

In your five minutes of quiet time try saying to yourself lightly and easily: 'I am fine as I am.' Keep saying it, even though you may feel totally at odds with the line. Begin to inject a sense of reality into yourself so as to develop and move forward in your negotiating. Say this to yourself, not just in your head, but out loud whenever you have the chance and at least twenty or thirty times a day. It may take a couple of years for you even to begin to believe it, but it is a start. At home write it on 'post-it' notes or put another self-affirming line wherever your eyes frequently rest—on the telephone, the toilet, the bathroom cabinet, the kettle, or by your bedside—so that you are constantly reminded that you are fine as you are. After a few weeks or months add the line, 'this means . . . ' and listen to whatever thought comes to mind as you say it.

■ *This means...*

The implications for taking on this line are enormous and vary widely. For example:

- Am I wearing the sort of clothes I feel comfortable in? Which of my ideal clothes can I bring into my working situation? What can I do with my clothes that more appropriately reflects me?

- Am I eating the food that I most enjoy and is best for me? What could I eat more of or less of to regain a balance of energy in my life?

- Am I drinking fluids that make me feel good? For every four cups of coffee from the machine at work, how about taking a couple of tumblers of water, or next time in the sandwich bar pick up a litre of fruit juice as well.

- What about my hair? Is it the way I want? Does it need cutting?

- Am I as fit as I want to be? If not, what am I going to do about it ? Walking one stop on the underground or parking the car further away and walking the last 200 yards will all improve your fitness.

You don't have to prove anything to anyone else. There is no need to be competitive, aggressive, or to win at the expense of someone losing—elements that prevail widely in competitive organisations— you can relax. Relaxing does not mean that changes will not take place, in fact the reverse is likely. A greater sense of self-esteem will probably lead to more changes rather than less, since you will feel more confident. Without negative self-criticism the changes will happen from a position of strength, not weakness.

Rackham and Carlisle

In *The Effective Negotiator* Neil Rackham and John Carlisle, of the Huthwaite Research Group investigated the strategy and skills that successful negotiators used. Their definition of a skilled negotiator was:

- they should be rated as effective by both sides;
- they should have a track record of significant success;
- they should have a low incidence of implementation failures.

They produced some interesting findings on the differences between skilled and average negotiators. These included:

In planning, skilled negotiators

- more often explored common ground between the parties involved.

- explored a wider bargaining range rather than the parties focusing on a fixed point or a particular issue.

- planned issues separately rather than in a predetermined sequence. So where a contract included a number of different issues, these were planned individually and the strategy for each worked out separately.

In behaviour, skilled negotiators

- sought information more by asking questions;

- summarised and tested understanding more often;

- avoided using irritators such as 'a generous offer', 'We are being fair in...';

- the only occasion where average negotiators used behaviour labelling more often was in signalling disagreement: such as 'Returning to your point about the contract, I would disagree on the basis that...', 'I want to clarify a point you made earlier...', 'Let me suggest something here...'. Average negotiators disagreed and then gave the reasons why. Skilled negotiators did the reverse.

- gave more comments on feelings, for example 'I am concerned about your suggestion on the basis that...', 'I am delighted about what we have achieved so far', 'I think we're reaching an impasse here. I suggest we adjourn for half an hour to see how we can move on.'

- avoided spirals of defend and attack. The following would not take place: 'Printing in blue-black sounds fine in principle but previously when orders have come through, the colour is neither one nor the other.' 'Well we always get copy from you at least ten days later than agreed so it makes our job impossible.'

- when attacks were made they were fast and tough. Skilled negotiators used fewer not more reasons to support the case, unlike average negotiators, who used more and so diluted their case.

- made immediate counter proposals, (responded to a proposal with another proposal) much less often than average negotiators.

So now that we are in top form, planned and prepared, we will move on to deal with the different ways of communicating in negotiating in person, by telephone and by letter.

6 The Means of Negotiating

You are your own best model.

Best method

As part of your planning, think about the best method of negotiating for you. With a new or difficult client—aggressive, dismissive, patronising—an initial letter followed up with a telephone call may be the most suitable and effective beginning. All of the means we use have consequences.

Whether you negotiate by letter, telephone or in person it is you that will be travelling down the telephone line or appearing on paper. The image we give of ourselves is a very powerful model and easily the most effective resource we have to use in a negotiation. Let's look in more detail at the differing ways that you can carry out your negotiation.

Negotiating in person

This is by far the easiest way of reading the other person's responses to a proposal or suggestion both verbally and non-verbally. It also gives you the most means to communicate what you want.

Research has shown that when meeting someone for the first time, the way we communicate falls into three main categories:

- 6 per cent is communicated by the words that are used.

- 38 per cent is communicated by the tone, pitch and inflexion of the voice.

- 56 per cent is communicated by what is not said, i.e non-verbal behaviour, such as facial expressions, mannerisms, appearance, physique, posture, etc.

From this it is clear that the greatest communication resource is in the one-to-one or face-to-face negotiation when all these aspects, particularly non-verbal behaviour, are present. The amount we communicate through what we don't say is worth enlarging upon. It is easy to think that when we speak or listen to someone we actually hear the words that are said and understand what is being meant. In practice this is rarely the case.

Consider the last occasion when you met someone for the first time. It may have been a new client, or a new member of the department. What are your memories of that person? Is it what he or she said or more the way in which it was said and their general appearance or impression? Research has shown that it is nearly always the latter.

■ *We hear what we want to hear*

We all possess selective hearing, that is we hear what we want to hear: for example details of a new project in the department, rumours of possible job changes and likely promotions, increases in budget that will allow for recruiting a new member of staff, etc. We tend not to hear what we do not want to hear. Consider a meeting where one person who is making a point consistently takes two or three times the amount of time needed to express it. What is likely to happen to the other members of the group when this person begins to speak? They switch off, possibly hearing the opening few comments and the last part when the voice raises to indicate the end of their point of view.

Negotiating by telephone

For many the telephone is the most widely used tool for negotiating and the most personal.

What is important here is to communicate interest, concern, commitment, passion, etc. Taking the above communication statistics into account, the telephone allows only 44 per cent of the total means available to communicate. If the biggest asset we have is ourselves, the question is how to get that extra 56 per cent down the telephone line.

Stand up or sit down

Try this simple exercise, preferably with a partner. Sit down and speak your name in as many different ways as possible. Now stand up, place your feet evenly on the ground about a foot apart, and imagine a string which is reaching from the top of your head to the base of your spine. Imagine that this string is slowly pulling you up from both these points. Let that happen and allow your shoulders to settle down into a comfortable position from the string. Let your hands fall by your side and release any muscles that are tense, working your way up from your toes through to your legs, torso, shoulders, arms, neck and face. Once your body is extended, allow your shoulders to move down a little and slightly back so you are opening up the diaphragm and the voice-box.

Now say your name again and in as many different ways as possible, and notice any difference between projecting your voice standing and sitting down. Whilst standing your voice will sound fuller and stronger. There is enormous power in our voices and it is this that needs to be projected down the telephone line to convey interest, concern or commitment. Stand whilst you make the telephone call. Not only will your voice be stronger but your call may well be shorter, and so will be more cost-effective.

■ *The sound of your own voice*

Discover how your voice sounds on the telephone by recording your side of the conversation on one of the next telephone calls that you make or receive. (It is illegal to record both sides of the call unless the other party knows and agrees to it.)

What is important here is to learn about the inflection, intonation and pitch of your voice. So listen both to what you are saying and the way in which you are saying it.

- Could it be more succinct and explicit?

- Are you repeating your offer unnecessarily?

- How many times did you say: 'Ah-ha', 'Yes', 'Um-hum', 'Ummm'?

- Do you interrupt the caller? (This conveys your impatience or suggests that you are not listening to their point of view.)

- Do you counter or acknowledge their point of view too early when they make a proposal that you disagree with?

- Do you finish your sentences? With face-to-face contact there are other aspects working on our behalf (visual image and facial expressions) and you can allow sentences to trail off without the main message being lost. On the telephone, however, clarity is essential.

- Does your voice drop or rise at the end of a sentence? Lowering it at the end can convey despondency, raising it can convey hope.

- What have you learnt about your voice and how could it be different?

■ *Breathing to calm down*

Before making the telephone call, if you are nervous repeat the standing position mentioned earlier in this chapter, weight evenly distributed between both feet and arms relaxed by your side. Slowly inhale and exhale three times to relax your breathing and to feel more centred.

What often happens under stress is that the pulse quickens, perspiration increases and we experience the 'fight or flight' response, that is we want to run away or to stand our ground and fight what appears to be the enemy. The reality is that you will survive this telephone call.

■ *Clothes*

It may seem strange to be discussing clothes to wear for negotiating on the telephone. However, the point has already been made of the value of clothes to our self-esteem and this applies whether or not we are visible. Having decided on the appropriate time to make the telephone call, wear clothes that make you feel at your best. What you wear reflects your self-image and a heightened sense of self-worth will communicate itself down the telephone line.

■ *The best time?*

Establish the best time for you to make a telephone call, and also what is likely to be the best time for the other party. Your preference may be for between 10.30 and 11.45 in the morning but if your call is to a factory supervisor, you may interrupt an urgent production run. Find out when is the best time to call and if necessary come to work earlier to make the call at 8.15. a.m. What you gain in good relations will more than outweigh an earlier start to the day.

> *'I'm calling to discuss the new contract. Is this a good time or shall I ring you back?'*

With transatlantic calls bear in mind time differences and likely work patterns and work schedules. It is perfectly acceptable to make a telephone call to establish a good time to discuss the negotiations. In your planning consider who is going to take the initiative on the telephone call. Initiating the call can be a more powerful strategy than picking up the receiver and wondering who is at the other end.

■ *You can always say 'no'*

Incoming calls often happen at the most unsuitable times. The tendency is to feel obliged to discuss the negotiation there and then. It is a powerful strategy to say, in effect: 'thanks but no.'

> *'I'm delighted you've phoned, I've been thinking that it's time to talk about the new contract. However, this isn't the best time. Can I call you back in half an hour?'*

Expect disappointments: the person you want may not be available, may have left the firm or be on holiday for the next week. However, looking good and feeling good will benefit your negotiating strategy in general, or other aspects of your work.

■ *Finally...*

An advantage in negotiating by telephone is that all your preparation work can be in front of you as you speak. The other party isn't to know that you are working between your ideal and realistic positions and with a list of alternative questions. In this respect, negotiating on the phone has a distinct advantage over working in person, when this information would often need to be in your head.

◼ Negotiating by fax or telex

Alternative forms of communicating are emerging all the time through technological developments and this will increase at an even faster rate in the years to come. The fax and telex system is a fast and efficient way of communicating. In addition to its speed it has a high probability of reaching the receiver's organisation, which cannot always be said of the letter. If speed is of the essence, a fax or telex can confirm very quickly all the agreements made in your telephone negotiation. This leads us on to the written word, where clarity and correctness are so important.

◼ Negotiating by letter

The written word can form all or a part of the negotiation. A letter or memo can follow up a meeting or telephone call or can be the sole mechanism through which the negotiation takes place. Sometimes the parties involved never meet or speak to one another so what is communicated on paper has to encompass both the technical content required and the meaning and impression the writer wants to convey.

In transcribing thoughts from the planning to the written word it is essential to do so lightly and clearly, as well as to convey your own personal style and include requests for information and action to the reader. In negotiating by letter you must:

- request action at the end;
- convey your personal style;
- keep it light and clear;
- avoid jargon.

> *The manager of a high street bank received a letter from an investor enquiring whether she could invest a sum of money in the name of her dog. The manager replied, addressing the letter to the dog itself and in dog-style language:*
>
> *Dear Rover,*
> *How are things down at the kennel? Chased any good rabbits lately? I'm delighted to hear that you are interested in saving with us. I hope you can buy some tins of good dog food and possibly a new kennel with the interest that we will pay on your investment.*
>
> *Three days later the manager received a cheque for £15,000.*

Taking a risk and really addressing the letter in person, couched with humour, can have positive and productive results.

It is much more difficult to convey all that is wanted using only the written word. It should be apparent by now that personal communication gives a far fuller picture of our requests as well as showing our own personal style. It also allows us the opportunity to respond to the other person as well as being able to really hear what the other party is saying.

■ *Style and language*

There has been a peculiar British tradition of lapsing into a sort of antiquarian prose when writing a letter or dictating. What we would say to the person face-to-face is transformed into another language.

For example, 'Thank you for', is replaced by, 'We thank you for', or 'We are in receipt of'. Many words that have entered the business language could be replaced by much more straightforward words.

I'm sure you are all too familiar with the following phrases:

- 'We have pleasure in...'
- 'In due course...'
- 'Herein...'
- 'Grateful to acknowledge receipt of...'
- 'With all due respect...'
- 'We remain yours...'

Write in a style familiar to the person reading the letter. If the style is not understood by the other party it can be off-putting and act as a deterrent to successful negotiation. Bear in mind language or cultural differences, particularly when you are negotiating with someone from another country.

■ *Addressing the other party*

Often I receive business mail (which I am reluctant to call 'junk' mail as obviously a great deal of thought and effort has gone into its production) which has my correct title on the envelope yet inside is addressed to 'Dear Madam' or even worse, 'Dear Sir/Madam'. Find out exactly who it is you are writing to and make sure the spelling of their name and title is correct. Grammar and language points may seem like a throwback to schooldays but spelling a person's name correctly is an important element in establishing a good working relationship.

Make sure your name is printed in full at the foot of a letter. Too often a letter is signed with an illegible scribble, so that it is difficult to know who to respond to. The result is that the correspondence has frustration already built in whilst you establish who the point of contact is. Bearing in mind that we are aiming for a stress-free negotiation, being clear about who you are and who you are negotiating with is a fundamental starting point.

■ *Layout*

Give your outgoing letter the 'early morning test'. Imagine your
letter arriving on the desk of the other party amidst a pile of
competing mail:

- What effect is it likely to have when he or she opens it
  up?
- Will it stand out from the other mail, and in what way?
- Is the layout attractive?
- Has the letter been well spaced throughout the page?
- Is the letter completely free of spelling and grammatical
  error?
- What information are you conveying and is it clear what
  you want?
- Does this letter make you feel uplifted?

Requests for action or information should be included in the last part
of the letter as it will be the first thing that the reader will remember.
If the letter contains a number of points for negotiation, such as the
various elements of a new contract, list these separately and clearly
on another page.

Kiss, kick, kiss

Invariably in a negotiation, there will be areas of disagreement,
difference and potential conflict. Remember that the issue is being
challenged, not the person. To make a negative point or challenge a
proposal, surround that point with positive comments, i.e. Kiss,
Kick, Kiss. For example:

Kiss

Acknowledge a point of the proposal that you like. This may be the realistic delivery dates, the percentage discount, or that your appraisal interview will be in two, rather than four months' time.

Kick

Follow this with the source of your concern or disagreement, outlining it specifically, expressing your concerns and making a proposal. For instance, 'I am concerned about the percentage discount on orders over £20,000 and suggest we increase this by 3 per cent.'

Kiss

End the letter or that section with an uplift such as an acknowledgement of the progress that you have made so far, the fact that you are looking forward to the meeting to discuss terms next week or to continuing doing business with the other party. This last point will be the one that the reader remembers.

Remember that criticism is not an end in itself. Hold on to the bigger picture of what you are wanting from the negotiation and follow the criticism with a specific request for action. In that context, conflict is an interesting hurdle to be sorted out in the light of the bigger framework.

In this chapter we have considered some of the different tools used in communicating. The following short activity will focus your attention on some of the ones you are likely to use.

Activity Sheet 7

■ What form of negotiating do you generally most prefer?
Why?

■ In the negotiation you are entering, what is the most
appropriate means (personal contact, telephone, letter) to
use initially:

  • for you?
  • for the other party?

■ What other forms of communication could you use during
the negotiations?

7 Listening

'When the eyes say one thing and the tongue another, a practised one relies on the language of the first.'

(Hindustani proverb)

Total listening

Of all the skills used in negotiating, listening is the most central and the most challenging to demonstrate. Being able to listen well means being able to hear both the words that are said and also the message or the meaning behind those words, in other words, the music behind the notes. Listening well means being able to understand the full import of what is being said and to obtain the whole picture, so that it is possible to respond with the fullest amount of information at hand. It requires of the listener a mental, emotional and physical commitment to understanding what the other person is saying. This means not simply looking at the person whilst they are speaking, and conveying an interest, but also understanding what they are saying, from their point of view rather than your own.

To listen well is one of the most demanding activities a person can take part in and it is worth bearing in mind that professional listeners such as counsellors or therapists rarely give one-way listening time to another person for longer than 50 minutes. It is sometimes said that to listen for longer than 12 minutes is especially difficult for an audience. Notice how a professional speaker at a seminar will vary the means of delivery to include visual aids or movement from the platform in order to retain the interest of the audience. Young people in a classroom are a powerful example of how hard it is to listen for any considerable length of time.

Improving listening skills

What is covered in this chapter is how to listen well to the other party in order to fully understand their proposal in the negotiation. As already mentioned, many of the skills included in negotiating are part of our everyday life. In particular this includes listening, which we have been practising all our lives in different ways. What is considered here is how to improve listening skills and to overcome the blocks that prevent listening effectively.

To return to the image of the iceberg: the first chapters have been concerned with the strategy and the planning of the negotiation (90 per cent of the iceberg submerged beneath the water). The tip of the iceberg is the negotiation itself, and I estimate that 75 per cent of this tip involves active listening and 25 per cent communicating ideas, proposals, suggestions, alternatives and what you want from the negotiation. There is a saying from the *Tao Te Ching*:

'Those who know do not speak, those who speak do not know.'

This may seem rather severe, but I would encourage you to consider its implications.

The rehearsal curve

Have there been times in meetings when you have listened to one person spend several minutes making a point and wondered at the end just what it was they were trying to say? What happens when this pattern is repeated frequently is that the listener begins to switch off after the first few moments of the opening comment and the pattern of thought is something like the following diagram.

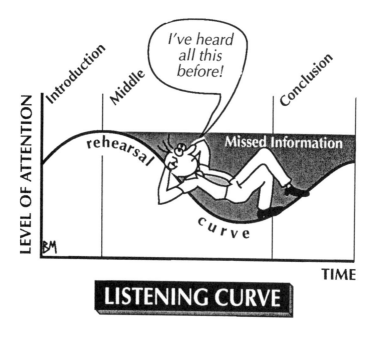

LISTENING CURVE

With people who meet often, for example, in departmental meetings or project groups, patterns or norms arise between the members. We know for instance that Bill will remain very quiet throughout the meeting but when he does speak, the others know that his point will be relevant and will listen to him. Other patterns can arise in a different way. Meanwhile, when Sam speaks there is an expectation that he will spend several minutes making a point that could be said in ten seconds and the group gets irritated while waiting for him to finish. Invariably one person (it may be the same person) will interrupt him part-way through his contribution. It is much harder to listen than to speak, yet if we are unable to listen well the value of what is spoken is lost.

The listening curve illustrated above shows how our level of attention rises and falls within a certain space of time and depending on who it is that we are listening to. The time axis could be a few moments or a few minutes. When someone starts to speak our attention is high or is raised whilst we find out what they are going to speak about. It may be a revised offer for a contract, or information about a new post that has become vacant in the department, or that the vendor of the house you want has received your offer.

Once the essence of what the speaker is going to say is known, the level of attention of the listener can diminish, as illustrated in the diagram, particularly if we have heard this type of remark from the speaker before. For example, the client in a negotiation has acknowledged the proposal for an increase in price for the regular order. He or she then moves on to explain the difficult position their company is in, that trade is falling, jobs are being lost and his or her hands are tied. It is at this point that the level of listening attention is likely to fall down. However, it is exactly at this point of awareness that interest is falling that the listener needs to retain the horizontal level of attention so that any important elements that might come out are not missed. Where the level of attention slides down is called a 'rehearsal curve', that is, our mind says something such as: 'I have heard this all before and I know what he or she is going to be saying next so I shall switch off.' What is important in listening actively is to hear what the speaker is saying as though this is the first time this piece of information is being said. This is what makes listening the most challenging process in our communication with others.

Being in a position to listen well

This means that you have put the time aside to have your conversation. There must be a minimal number of interruptions by colleagues and no time pressures like an imminent meeting. Where possible, put an engaged sign on your door or desk to show that you do not want to be interrupted. Do not look at anyone who happens to come into your room whilst you are on the telephone and, where appropriate, indicate to colleagues, particularly if you work in an open-plan office, that you do not want to be disturbed for the next ten minutes.

Listening well means that you have created the right atmosphere for you to listen to one another well. It includes many of the areas mentioned above, including having a meeting room conducive to discussion without interruption. It particularly means having cleared your head of any issues that are likely to interfere with your ability to listen. So imminent crises at work have been deflected or postponed, or someone else is dealing with them.

It means having seating and an atmosphere conducive to talking to one another and making the setting as welcoming as possible. Again it means having no interruptions, either by other people or by telephones, and taking the view that this time between you—be it a few minutes or a few hours—is of prime importance to the negotiation. The planning and preparation you have invested in it merits a time of quality.

■ *Listening actively*

Listening actively means communicating in both a verbal and non-verbal way that you are interested in the other person. By this I mean it is important to look at the other person with relaxed and easy eye contact (not staring at them unblinkingly) and to display an easy and open posture. Sitting back in your chair, arms folded and looking frequently over the other person's shoulder or out of the window is hardly likely to convey an aura of interest.

"We were really looking for someone who was a better listener."

It is easy to appear interested by sitting upright or slightly forward in the chair, both feet evenly on the ground, palms relaxed in the lap and looking at the other person. At the same time, mentally the listener is miles away, maybe thinking about the meeting coming up in half an hour's time or the work that still needs to be done in preparation for it. Or maybe about a row with their partner before leaving for work this morning or the ill-health of a family member.

Any number of issues can affect the listener and his or her ability to listen well. What is important in listening fully is being both physically and mentally in tune and attentive so that whatever else is going on in the mind of the listener, for that moment in time, all that is important is understanding what it is the other person is saying.

■ *Listening well means suspending judgement*

Each of us has an inherent set of beliefs and values that have grown over the years and that we act out in our daily life. These are the product of our upbringing, family, education and peers. However, they have no place at the moment we are listening to another person. This is not to deny their importance—they are of central importance to ourselves. Yet we must put these beliefs to one side, particularly if they form a prejudice or a block to our hearing.

For example it may be that in aiming to reduce the price the other party includes in the argument a criticism of your company's operation. Being criticised can prevent us hearing the content of the argument, and our own responses—pride in our workplace, valuing a product of the organisation, believing in the work we are doing and so on—can serve only to fuel our own arguments and denigrate the other person's argument. Either way it prevents us from listening to the essence of their proposal.

The aim in listening well is to remain as open as possible to proposals and arguments.

■ *Listening well involves respect*

Respect the fact that the other party has a right to their point of view, even though you may fundamentally disagree with it. This re-emphasises the importance of respecting the person and what they are aiming to achieve, whilst challenging the arguments or proposals they are suggesting.

■ *Listening well involves being light*

Many of the issues that confront us at work, including those that involve negotiations, assume a weight and importance of their own. Sometimes the weight is inappropriate: the situation becomes very serious and heavy. Retain a view that although the situation is important and deserving of respect and attention, it doesn't have to be too serious. The aim of this approach is to free the thinking and attention of all parties. When things are desperate in organisations, a line I offer is: 'The situation is hopeless, but not serious.' This often causes laughter and some relief of the tension. For as long as we are steeped in the heaviness of the situation, we cannot influence it well.

■ *Listening well is communicating*

Communicate verbally that you are listening. A number of skills are important here:

(a) Summarising

This is the ability to extract the essence of what has been said and restate it simply in a line or phrase. Particularly where the other party is covering a number of issues, this ability can be of immense value. There is a tendency to assume that summarising is useful only at the end of a conversation, for example in terms such as, 'To sum up then...', or 'Let me summarise what we have agreed so far...'. Whilst this strategy is of great value, there is no need to leave it until the end. Where the negotiation involves a number of issues, as with a contract, summarise each aspect before you move on to the next area for negotiation. Summarising is a useful way of checking that both parties are clear about the issues. Whilst you think you are summarising for your own benefit, in fact you are clarifying the situation for both of you. It is another way of checking that both of you agree about the issue under discussion. If it isn't clear, the other party will soon reply, 'Well no, that wasn't what we agreed', or 'That isn't what I understood. What I thought we had agreed was...'. Each of you then has the opportunity to clarify the situation before moving on. So as a general rule, summarise often, particularly at the beginning of a negotiation and in negotiations of complexity.

(b) Reflecting

This is the skill of playing back in your own words what you have heard the other person say. Reflecting is the result of listening well and being able to summarise. Like garlic, a little goes a long way, and whilst it may seem initially an unwieldy practice, you cannot go wrong. If you have inadvertently missed the point, the other party will soon put you right and if you have 'hit the spot' the other party will be delighted. So basically you can't lose by reflecting, using phrases such as :

- 'It seems that...'
- 'You feel that...'

(c) Clarifying

This is a valuable skill in negotiating, particularly in identifying the issues. For example:

- 'So you have a meeting finishing at 6 o'clock on Thursday when I'm away and there is no one to pick up the children?'

- 'So what you're saying is this new equipment which will shorten the print run won't be available until November?'

(d) Checking understanding

As the phrase implies, this is simply a way of clarifying that you have heard what the other person has said and communicating that. The very act of checking also confirms that what has been said is important. This checking can be demonstrated through clarifying, reflecting or summarising.

Summary

The aim of using these skills is to ensure that both parties are clear about the issues at hand. As with all skills of negotiating and interacting, use them when they are real and of value. By this I mean that there are often rituals and 'games' that are played in the process of negotiation. Ask questions, clarify, summarise or reflect when you genuinely need to clarify the situation and gain some more information. Finally, although this comment is obvious, it is one which is easy to overlook:

'If the situation to be negotiated is not clear at the beginning, the rest of the negotiation will go beautifully awry.'

Levels of listening

In addition to all of these skills, listening well involves being aware of the different levels that occur when listening to another person.

■ Head level

At its simplest level, when listening to another person we listen at what can be called an 'intellectual' or 'head level'. That is we speak, aiming to communicate as far as possible what we want and mean, and we listen to what the other person has to say. This is a relatively straightforward interaction of communication between two people.

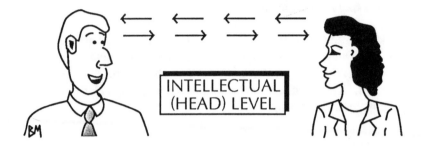

INTELLECTUAL (HEAD) LEVEL

■ *Feelings level*

There is another level that operates in interaction and that can affect the level of listening. This is the level of the feelings that arise between two people which may be positive—delight, with humour and so on—or negative—including concern, fear, aggression, ambition, dismissiveness. In organisations, the feelings that arise between the boss and subordinates, or between colleagues, are rarely if ever acknowledged. This can be appropriate, though not always. If negative feelings between two colleagues are not acknowledged and resolved, their performance at work on a departmental project will severely impair the success of the outcome. At other times it may be inappropriate to acknowledge feelings of, say, attraction or hostility if to do so would have a dysfunctional effect upon the departmental membership.

What is important in listening is to be aware of the feelings that the other person raises within us and to explore within ourselves, or with the help of a trusted friend, the source of those feelings and the value of making them open in your negotiation.

To some of you the acknowledgement of such feelings may seem alien. You may be thinking: 'What on earth has this to do with negotiating?' Well let me say: 'A lot.' We all have feelings and, to differing extents, are able to acknowledge them to ourselves and to others. This will often depend on the level of safety and trust between ourselves and the other person. For many in organisations, the safety is highest when we are with those outside our work, family and close friends. In negotiations, depending on whether they are at work or home based, our feelings can help or get in the way.

So in your negotiation, consider how you feel about the other person quite separately from the issues you are negotiating:

- How do you feel about working with this person?

- What do you respect/like/admire about them?

- What do you find most challenging about them?

- Is there a part of the negotiation where it would be appropriate for you to comment on the feelings that you have? For example to say: 'I am concerned about this particular aspect of the contract', or: 'I always look forward to renegotiating our contract with you. It is always a challenge, yet good fun.'

■ *Helicoptering*

This is another level of listening. It involves the ability to maintain all the elements of active listening that have been mentioned, as well as mentally having almost a third eye which is hovering above the conversation, the meeting or the telephone conversation and observing the negotiation as it develops. Helicoptering resembles a video camera watching the whole process. Your 'third eye' is the camera. Imagine what it would be recording if it were plugged on the wall watching the interaction. Questions that may be raised using this technique might be:

- Are there issues that are not being addressed, for instance the late delivery of the supplies last month, or the fact that the invoice was three months in being paid?

- Is the conversation moving towards the elements of the negotiation you have prepared, or has the conversation wandered off down another alley which is irrelevant to the present discussion?

■ *Seeing the whole*

Helicoptering is the part that distinguishes hearing from real or active listening, for it demands that you maintain contact with the other person, respond and initiate, whilst at the same time being able to beam up and view the conversation as a whole. This observation is then used as a feedback mechanism with which to plan your next question. It may be that during the meeting you have noticed the

other person sitting rather slumped in the chair; their voice is quite low and their eyes avoid yours when you mention your proposal. Verbally the response from the other party may be positive: 'I can agree to that', they say. Yet their body language or non-verbal behaviour conveys a very different message. What do you do? Two options are open. You can act on what is said and move the negotiation forward, or you can use your observation to ask a question such as:

'You say you can accept the offer, which naturally I am delighted about. Are you sure you are quite happy with this?'

By this intervention you are acknowledging the present moment—what is actually happening—as well as conveying that you have heard what the other person has said. You also show that you are aware of *how* it has been said, which is the essence of active listening. To listen well is to be able to listen on all three levels simultaneously. This is why professional listeners do it for a relatively short period of time. Try out the following exercises, some of which can be done on your own or with a partner, a colleague or a friend whom you trust.

Activity Sheet 8

- Speaker A talks for two minutes on any subject (last holiday, the weekend, Christmas, most liked/disliked aspects of work).
  Listener B, without speaking, conveys non-listening by any means that come to mind (looking away, stance, gestures etc.)
  After two minutes ask these questions of each of you:

- Speaker A: What was it like to be listened to in this way?
- Listener B: What was it like listening in this way?

- Speaker A talks on any subject for two minutes.
  Listener B verbally communicates non-listening by interrupting or talking about something else. After the two minutes ask:

- Speaker A: What was it like to be listened to in this way?
- Listener B: What was it like to listen in this way?

- Individually
  Next time you are in a meeting or conversation, watch what the other person does to convey:
  - listening
  - not listening

- What do *you* do to convey:
  - listening?
  - not listening?

- What could be different?

Activity Sheet 9

■ In pairs:

A speaks for one minute on any subject.
B listens and summarises what has been said.
Discuss how effective the summary was.

This activity can also be done on your own. In a meeting or conversation, practise summarising periodically what has been said and check how effective the summary has been.

■ In pairs:

A speaks for one minute on a chosen topic.
B listens and clarifies or checks understanding of what has been said.
Discuss the effectiveness of the clarification.

8 Using Questions

question, kwes'chan, n.—an inquiry; an interrogation; the putting of a problem; a demand for an answer; an interrogative sentence or other form of words in which it is put.

In its naivest form a question is any sentence which has a verbal or written question mark at the end of it. So it could be a sentence or even a word which prompts further information from the person being questioned. For example: 'Really?', or repetition of a phrase that the other person has said, such as: 'Business is slowing down?' can provide a question.

We shall look at the different types of question and their effect in a moment. The main reason to use questions is:

- to elicit information;
- to focus the discussion;
- to establish rapport;
- to reorientate the discussion;
- to move the discussion forward.

What follows is information on the different types of question, their usefulness and structure, as well as examples. When asking questions it is important to consider both what is being asked and how it is being asked. The content of the question—i.e. whether it is an open or a closed one—will be communicated by the vocal expression, mannerisms and facial expressions of the person asking the question.

Types of question

Questions fall into one of two main types: open and closed.

■ *Open questions*

Open questions are for eliciting information and are particularly useful when:

- gathering information;
- drawing out a quiet person.

They typically begin with one of a number of words such as 'what', 'how', 'who', 'where' or 'why'. If a question begins with one of these words it is very difficult to respond in a monosyllable, so they are particularly useful at the beginning of a discussion and in the opening comments of your negotiation. For example:

- 'How are things at work?'
- 'What has happened as a result of the takeover ?'

Bear in mind who you are asking the question of. An open question asked of a talkative person may occupy ten minutes of a tightly timed meeting so an alternative question, such as a direct or closed one, may elicit the same amount of information but in a shorter way.

Returning to open questions, 'what' and 'how' are the two most often used. For example:

- 'What has been happening since I last saw you?'
- 'How are things?'
- 'How are we getting on?'
- 'What do we need to do today?'
- 'What needs to happen now?'

- 'How can we best move forward?'
- 'What would be an ideal outcome?'
- 'Where would you most like to go on holiday?'
- 'Where do you see yourself working in two years' time?'
- 'Who can best help us with this contract?'
- 'Who else is involved in the house chain?'
- 'Why do you think this happened?'
- 'Why will it take six weeks and not four?'
- 'Why am I not being promoted?'

A word of caution about the use of questions beginning 'why?' They tend to elicit an intellectual or head-level response, which may be perfectly appropriate for your discussions. However if a richer or fuller response is required, a question beginning with 'what?' may be more useful. For example, in the question, 'Why will it take six weeks?', an alternative is: 'What is happening in the department for the delivery to take six weeks and not four?' or 'What will prevent the delivery happening in four weeks rather than six?'

▪ *Closed questions*

These are useful for:

- direct, straightforward 'yes' or 'no' replies;
- confrontation.

Closed questions are a valuable strategy with talkative people. They are likely to respond quite fully, even to a closed question, but maybe not as much as to an open question. For example: 'Do you want to go house hunting on Saturday?', 'Can you deliver by Monday of next week?' They can be powerful techniques to use in confronting a situation, for example: 'Do you still want to do business with us?'

These questions are more appropriate during the middle stages of a conversation or negotiation rather than at the beginning, when confrontation might impair the rapport.

■ *Direct questions*

Direct questions are similar to closed questions and are useful for gathering facts and information where the reply is likely to be a word or phrase rather than a 'yes' or a 'no'. For example:

- 'When will the car be ready to collect?'
- 'How long am I to work on this project?'
- 'Do you want a cup of tea?'
- 'When will the proposal be ready?'
- 'Shall we meet on Monday or Tuesday?'

These gather specific information, and serve as a balance to open questions. A combination of an open question followed by a direct question is useful. For example: 'What are the company's plans for next year? When do you expect flotation?'

■ *Probing questions*

Probing questions are used for:

- finding out more information about a topic that has been raised;
- communicating that you have been listening.

Probing questions can either be questions in their own right, for example: 'Can you say some more about that?' or they may be a restatement of a word or phrase just mentioned, with the addition of a question mark, for example: 'Expansion?' or 'A new system coming in?'

■ Linking questions

Linking questions are useful for:

- communicating that you have heard an earlier point;
- developing continuity and moving the negotiation forward.

Here are some examples: 'Earlier you mentioned that the author is planning another book in this series. Can you say some more about that?' 'You mentioned that there are going to be changes in Accounts. What form are these likely to take?'

To ask a linking question, acknowledge the point in the other person's conversation that you are referring to; ask a question of your own. This may be an open or direct question. What is characteristic of using linking questions is that you are referring back to a point made earlier in order to move the discussion on.

■ Hypothetical questions

Hypothetical questions are used to envisage possibilities and explore alternatives. They are especially useful when the negotiation has reached an impasse or when the other party may be unable to consider alternative options or specific aspects of your proposal. The effect of a hypothetical question is to alter the situation to one with more possibilities. These are the questions to use when you have hit the brick wall in the negotiation. For example:

- 'If there was a solution to this problem, what do you think it would be?'
- 'What would you most like to be doing in your work?'
- 'If we had found a good way of doing business together what would it look like?'

Hypothetical questions are particularly useful for joint problem-solving.

Questions to avoid

There are some questions which can hinder the negotiation:

■ *Leading questions*

In these the answer is implied in the way the question is asked. For example: 'Well that's not the way we do it here, is it?' Leading questions simply confirm what the questioner wants to hear. They will not provide open information, so treat the replies with extreme caution and be aware when you are being asked a leading question.

■ *Fixed-choice questions*

Here the respondent is given one of two alternatives. These questions can be useful for simplifying the information at hand and selecting key elements for discussion in a negotiation. For example:

- 'Will you take delivery on Tuesday or Friday?'
- 'Do you want tea or coffee?'

The disadvantage of fixed-choice questions is, as the term implies, that the choice is limited to two options. There may be other alternatives which have not been considered and so the choice is unnecessarily restricted. Use with care.

■ *Multiple-choice questions*

This is where two or more questions are asked simultaneously. For example:

- 'What do you think about the situation in Bosnia? Do you think ... or ...?'

- 'What do you think about 1992 and the free market entry into Europe? Has it benefitted UK businesses or should more have been done to, say, teach German and French to staff?'

In these examples three questions have been asked. The likelihood is that the respondent will reply to the last one, since that will be the one freshest in their mind. Multiple-choice questions serve mainly to confuse. Think about what you are wanting from the respondent and consider what other type of question—say a direct or probing question—would elicit a more useful response.

Listen to interviewers on the radio and television. Often they ask a multiple-choice question beginning with an open one and following with a fixed-choice or direct one. For example:

- 'How do you feel about the Sunday opening of shops?' 'Do you think that traders should be allowed to sell or is it another example of the loss of religion in this country?'

The questions are often strategic: the interviewer will want a brief and succinct reply to the question, bearing in mind the short time available and the medium being used, so the open question sets the scene. However that isn't the question the interviewer wants a reply to for it would take too long. Instead, he or she follows it up with a fixed-choice or direct question which limits the respondent's reply and will hopefully keep it short. Next time you watch the television or listen to the radio, listen to the way in which the interviewers ask questions and see into which categories the questions fall. Also note the effect of the question on the respondent.

Activity Sheet 10

Listen to a radio or television interviewer.

■ What types of question are being asked?

■ What effect do the questions have on the other person?

■ In your own negotiation, what types of question will be useful:

   • at the beginning

   • in the middle

   • at the end

■ Give two examples of each that you can use.

9 Conflict

Rule number 1: 'Don't sweat the small stuff.'
Rule number 2: 'It's all small stuff.'
Rule number 3: 'When you can't fight and you can't flee, flow.'

(Robert Eliot, 1983)

Conflict is an inherent part of everyday life and of negotiating. It would be a rare negotiation that did not have elements of disagreement and variants which can lead to conflict. Some would say that by definition negotiation involves conflict, since at least two parties are competing for an outcome and bringing with them interests which can be at odds with one another.

So expect that in negotiations there will at some stage be conflict, and welcome it. There are strategies for both diagnosing and dealing with conflict that resolve the situation without leaving either party feeling bad.

Conflict does *not* necessarily mean:

- that your proposal is no good;
- that you're no good;
- that the other party is no good;
- that she/he doesn't like me;
- that communication has broken down;
- the end of the negotiation.

Conflict is simply an interesting hiccup in the path towards a realistic outcome and it can be dealt with swiftly and lightly.

▆▆▆▆▆▆ What is the source of the conflict?

It is essential to find out the exact source of the problem before applying any sort of solution to it. Otherwise it would resemble sticking a piece of plaster to the wrong wound. Inherent in this is the strategy of asking questions, a technique covered in Chapter 8. Questions such as: 'What's the problem here?', 'We seem to be hitting a brick wall over this issue. Can we stop and look at what we have agreed and clarify what the problem is?' Ask. Ask. Ask. The pursuit of information and clarification will serve both to identify the problem and to communicate to the other party that you too are committed to resolving the issue.

Through the skills mentioned in Chapter 8—asking questions, clarifying, checking understanding, reflecting—establish the exact source of the conflict.

There are two likely reasons for conflict. It can be a legitimate or actual issue, such as the price being too high or the time scale too long or too short, or a lack of understanding. Both of these above examples can be resolved by questioning and listening effectively.

The other source of conflict may be an issue not between the two parties but within one of you. That is, the negotiations may be triggering feelings which are entering the negotiation and hindering it. Imagine a negotiation where the other party is forceful, dominant, clear about what she wants, tenacious and dismissive both of your arguments and frequently of yourself as a person. Check how you feel. Angry? Aggressive? Demolished? And who does this person remind you of? Your mother? Your old boss?

People and situations can remind us of other events and experiences which have had an important effect upon us at the time, and this can then trigger positive or negative feelings. These feelings are legitimate and real, but sometimes old experiences and the feelings associated with them can crop up in the least expected or wanted situations, such as in an important negotiation. It is important to recognise what is an old and remembered feeling and what is the reality of the present occasion. If the other party in the negotiations reminds you that this is exactly how your mother behaved when you were a child, tell yourself that this is not your mother and this is not your childhood. This is now and a completely new situation.

Feelings are important, legitimate and real. Sometimes however, they have no place in negotiations so in analysing the source of conflict it is important to realise whether the nature of the conflict is an old feeling to do with a previous experience, or whether it is caused by the present situation.

◼ Dealing with conflict

If the source of conflict is an issue for the other person, use the skills mentioned in Chapter 8—particularly those of questioning and listening—to clarify the problem.

If the source of the conflict is an issue for you, a number of strategies are available:

◼ *Quiet time*

Take time out to think and reflect on the situation. Writing is helpful, as the process of writing makes it easier to be objective. Write down your thoughts, feelings, attitudes, views—anything in fact that will assist you to clarify the situation and how to progress the negotiation.

◼ *Talk it through*

Take some uninterrupted time to talk through both the successes to date, and the immediate problems, with a trusted colleague or friend. Use the other person as a sounding-board and ask him or her simply to listen to you for two or three minutes whilst you clarify your thoughts. Ask them not to give their opinions or advice or to question you, unless it is for clarification. What you need here is someone who will beam at you delightedly whilst you talk about the disaster that has happened. The aim is to clarify your thinking for yourself and to identify the best next step.

■ *Dump the feelings*

If the source of the conflict is feelings within yourself, use whatever resource is available to get rid of these feelings, whether they are positive or negative. Do whatever is best for you. Physical exercise is a valuable and a highly effective release of emotion, particularly pent-up anger, and if anger or any other feeling is getting in the way of the negotiations it is important to let that out.

Cushions and pillows are excellent receivers of physical abuse. They don't fight back, they don't hurt you and they are also good for yelling into without disturbing the neighbours. Yell. Releasing the emotion vocally is another strategy. Be thoughtful about yourself, the environment and other people: this is not for doing whilst you are in the office, driving (you need your concentration) or for walking in the park with the dog. If you do have a mountain to yourself or a swimming pool where you can yell underwater, try it out, making sure to shout from the base of your stomach and not from your throat or you will damage your vocal cords. Aim for the deepest sound, like a roar, and think of the person who is causing you all this frustration while you do it.

The point to emphasise when dealing with conflict is that it is rarely a good idea to give vent to the feelings of anger, frustration or aggression to the person concerned: the result would be that the discussion then revolves around dealing with the anger instead of the content of the negotiation itself. Separate out the feeling from the actual situation.

A word of warning. Under stress a classic reaction is to bury our feelings by compulsive eating, smoking or drinking alcohol. If you want to operate effectively in the negotiation don't expect any of these strategies to have any long-term benefits. At some stage you are going to need to deal with the reality of the conflict and sort it out. Assume that you can do it. Alcohol provides only a temporary boost by numbing our feelings.

■ Dealing with criticism

The nature of criticism falls into one of two areas:

- It is justified.
- It is unjustified.

Decide which area the criticism falls into and whatever the source, the response is always the same:

■ *Listen well*

Listen well using all the strategies mentioned in Chapter 7.

■ *Acknowledge*

Acknowledge that you have heard the other person's concerns and understood them. This does *not* mean coming out with stock phrases such as, 'I hear what you're saying', or 'I can understand why you feel like that...'. Phrases such as this can convey more that you have read a book on assertiveness or on dealing with criticism, rather than that you really see the other person's point of view. In all dealings be authentic. Bullshit is transparent, and people in organisations everywhere are generally tired of 'games'.

■ *Suggest a way forward*

Remember that conflict is an indicator that all is not well in the negotiation. It is insufficient simply to agree that conflict has arisen and that both of you have different positions over a particular issue. What is central is to acknowledge the difference and propose a route forward.

■ *Check whether the proposal is acceptable to the other party*

Look for both verbal and behavioural agreement, i.e that both the eyes and the body language are saying, 'yes', or 'no' or 'maybe'.

Throughout the whole of this section the value of listening cannot be overestimated.

Activity Sheet 11

- What types of situation do you find uncomfortable? List these.

- What types of people do you find difficult and challenging? List these.

- How do you usually deal with this type of situation or person?

- How else could you deal with this type of situation or person?

Activity Sheet 12

Sources of conflict

Conflict can arise for many different reasons. See if any of the following apply to your situation:

- I do not understand him/her

- I do not like him/her

- I do not like myself

- I don't want to be doing this

- I am too young

- I am too old

- He/she is bigger than me

- He/she is louder than me

- He/she is the wrong gender

- He/she is the wrong race

- He/she has insufficient technical information

- He /she doesn't speak the same language

10 Negotiating as part of a team

The focus of this book has been negotiating in person with one other party. There are times, however, when you may be negotiating as part of a departmental or cross-functional team and where this has implications both for the group dynamics and in the planning and the operation of the negotiation itself. This chapter looks at the aspects of negotiation that are affected by being a member of a team, and it enables you to operate effectively as a group member.

There can be joys and agonies in being a member of a group. On the up side you have support for your thinking, planning and the aftermath of the negotiation, there is lots of opportunity for fun and enjoyment and you have other people's thinking adding to your own, which can enrich the whole process and add creativity and freshness to your plans. By the very fact that you are part of a group, you are combating the isolation inherent in everyday work, especially in breaking new ground and embarking on new projects. There is much to be said for working with others all our working lives; even if the action we take is on our own, there is always a place for good and supportive allies.

On the down side, being part of a group brings its own challenges. Discussions and decisions take time, and personalities are part of the process, which can be helpful or unhelpful. How on earth to manage group negotiating so that the aims are achieved and the group members feel enhanced and uplifted?

Before moving on to the implications of negotiating in a group, here are a few questions to consider:

■ *Is this the best possible way of negotiating?*

Even if the negotiations for, say, the renewal of a contract have been carried out in this way for a number of years, keep asking yourself this question so that you can contribute fresh thinking. It may be that representatives of sales, marketing and production have always been involved. Does this work? If not, review the situation and see if there is some other way of gathering the best thinking to achieve the best settlement for you and the company.

■ *What would be the best combination?*

Assuming that negotiating as a group is the best mechanism available, ask yourself again what would be the best combination of members to achieve the required outcome. Gather the resources that will make it work. I know this sounds easy and you may not be in a position to alter or affect a decision that has been made for you by your manager. Do whatever you can. Within the power that you have, even acknowledging the situation to yourself is a bold step forward. You have information, use it in whatever way is appropriate for you and others around you.

According to Rosabeth Moss Kanter in *Men and Women of the Corporation*, power is most effective when it is balanced between the members of the group and when the source of this power is based on information, expertise or competence. (See Chapter 3 for the different definitions of power.)

■ *Planning*

In planning the negotiation with your group, consider the following points:

- Who will I be working with?
- Will it be the same group throughout the negotiation?
- What is the balance of power within our group?

- Where are our strengths?
- What is likely to be a challenge in working together as a group?
- What decision(s) do we therefore need to make in order to operate well together?

- How many people are we likely to be negotiating with?
- Who are they?
- What is their balance of power?
- Where are we likely to agree/disagree?
- What do we need to be vigilant about?

OK. You have already done a great deal of the work involved, that is, anticipating how your own group, and that of the other party, will operate. The next stage is to plan the strategy of your negotiation within your own group.

Planning the strategy

All that has been mentioned so far comes into this planning stage: being clear about what is wanted from a negotiation, the source of power, the clarity of the strategy, the ideal, realistic and fallback positions within each of the areas to be negotiated, clarity about which way to conduct the negotiation (in person, by letter or telephone, or a combination of all three) and where the negotiation is to take place.

As well as all of the above, here are a few points to consider in your planning as a group:

- Allow more time than you think you will need for your planning.

- Over and above the planning of the strategy, the dynamics of a group take time, which does not happen when operating solo. Allow time for this. Whilst this may seem frustrating, if it is clear that working in a group is the preferred option, then the richness that a group effort can produce needs time to develop. Depending on the maturity and stage of the group's development, this can take moments or months.

Tuckman's model

A model I like to illustrate a group's development is that of Tuckman (Tuckman and Jensen, 1977) which proposes that groups go through a five-stage development:

■ *Forming*

This is the stage when group members get to know one another. They establish the behaviours that are acceptable and what the ground rules are. (In *Organisation Development* Woodcock and Francis call this 'ritual sniffing'.) This applies to both the task in hand and to how individuals will work with one another; the interpersonal dimension.

Frequently this stage is characterised by confusion and uncertainty whilst individuals establish what it will be like to be in this group and whether they want to be in it. Once the individuals consider themselves as members of the group the forming stage is complete.

■ *Storming*

This stage, as the name implies, is characterised by a high degree of conflict and thrashing around without clear direction or consensus. Energy can be high, with everybody talking at once and very little listening taking place. Conflict is usually directed within the group to issues of leadership and the group leaders.

Some groups remain at this stage and, if the internal conflicts are not resolved, will never move on to operating effectively together. Once the issues are worked through and resolved, the storming stage is complete.

■ *Norming*

This is the stage when group cohesion and identification is at its highest. There is a real sense of shared ownership and responsibility for the group's task. The stage is complete when the group accepts one agreed way of operating together.

■ *Performing*

This happens when the group has got its act together and is operating well, using its resources to maximum effect, with an awareness of group process, that is, what is happening within the group. The group now uses this awareness to reflect, learn and move forward. When a group gets to this stage, it is a joy. Members should be feeling delighted to be a part of the group, recognising that the output is far greater than the sum of the individuals present. An effective group is fun, has a clear awareness of its task and what needs to happen in order to achieve it. Group members are sure of their roles and can carry these out with flexibility, allowing the opportunity to reassess and realign the group.

■ *Adjourning*

As the term implies, this is the stage when the group ceases to exist as the task is finished; the negotiation, project, whatever. The ending may be sudden, as when the negotiation is complete, or the group may disintegrate slowly if the norms established no longer sustain it or if group members leave. As with any ending, I recommend some ritual that signifies the end of the event or the experience of being together so that members do not leave with 'unfinished business'.

The ending ritual could include:

- anchoring the successes and highlights;
- acknowledging the challenges and difficulties;
- identifying what was learnt through the time together as a group;
- clarifying what will be different next time both as a group and for each group member.

Think about this model in the planning groups that you are in. What stage of development is the group at? How can you best move it forward? Bear in mind that a group will develop from stage 1 through to stage 5, yet there is also a pendulum swing—groups are likely to return to earlier stages over different issues. For instance on a new issue, or where the membership has changed, a group is likely to return to the early stages; this is fine, so long as there is a continuing move forward.

A good start

When groups meet for a work purpose most people bring with them issues that are not central to the task under discussion, yet nevertheless are valid. These thoughts could be about the work that is left behind, a meeting later in the day, leaving the house that morning with ill-feeling with a partner or concern about a family member who is unwell. What is important at the beginning of any meeting is to enable each person speedily and easily to get their attention on to the matter at hand so as to utilise the time fully and benefit all those who are there.

One way is to swiftly go round the group and hear from each person briefly about one thing that has gone well recently. This may be a recent success at work or something connected with the meeting at hand, or that they have enjoyed, indeed anything that has been a good or new event in their lives. This helps a group to divert its attention from other issues as well as reminding everyone that good things do happen; it is particularly useful if the content of the meeting is likely to be tough. Another advantage is that it cuts through the tendency for a few people to dominate the conversation and for the quieter ones to remain silent for some, if not all, of the time.

▬▬▬▬ Clarify the agenda

This is an easy item to overlook. Bearing in mind the point that each person is likely to bring a whole range of issues and thoughts to the meeting, it is essential for one person to clarify the aim of the meeting and why everybody is there. Setting the agenda and getting an agreement on the task provides the springboard for the rest of the meeting. This is central to any meeting whether it is the planning meeting for the negotiation or the meeting connected to the negotiation itself.

■ *No one speaks twice before everyone has spoken once*

In discussions, it is easy to slip into patterned ways of operating. For example, certain people will speak and others won't, and one norm that can develop is that those that speak know. Despite appearances, this is not necessarily the case. Within the planning group, ensure that all group members have an opportunity to contribute. The quiet members should not have to wait for a gap in the proceedings (which rarely comes) in order to speak. At the same time the energy of the group needs to be maintained and nurtured. This rule of thumb ensures that each person's contribution is valid and wanted. If someone's contribution is not wanted, the question arises—why are they there in the first place? This approach cuts across hierarchy and the assumption that those placed higher in the organisation have more value and merit more air time than those lower down. In some cases this may well be true but it is important to recognise that each person in that group has a valuable part to play.

So everyone has the responsibility to make sure that each person speaks at least once before anyone speaks twice. Similarly, no one speaks four times until everyone has spoken three times. This might seem a petty approach but try it out in your planning group and see what happens. Whilst it may seem unwieldy at the beginning, after a while it becomes second nature and even if it isn't rigorously adhered to, the principle will ensure that each person can and does contribute.

End with a highlight

End the meeting with an acknowledgement of something that has gone well or is of benefit. As mentioned in the section on writing letters, the last thing that is said is the first thing that is remembered. Leaving the group with an acknowledgement of progress provides a platform for the work to be carried out. Time permitting, this could again be a brief go-round with each person saying in a line or phrase what has been useful about the meeting, noting a highlight or something they are looking forward to. Or one person could begin a review and invite comments from others. Make it brief and make it light, especially if the meeting has been tough and challenging. With a sense of little progress or frustration, it is important to include this activity even though it might appear 'soft'. The reality is that even in tough meetings good things have happened. Although it may seem that the group is at the bottom of a well, reminding oneself and one another of the small inroads that have been made provides a rung or two out of the well. Do it, even if it feels uncomfortable, and watch the faces of the group. It is surprising how remembering a small positive contribution can lift the spirit; eyes begin to shine again, even if only for a moment. That is the basis on which movement can be made.

Planning the strategy of your group

Planning is the same, whether you are planning to negotiate by yourself or on behalf of a group. With a group negotiation there may be some additional points to consider. Here are some of them to add to the planning you would do in a solo negotiation.

■ *Who does it?*

Which members of the group will actually carry out the negotiation and how many will be involved? Will it be the same pair/trio etc. for the negotiation and, if not, who will begin, who will follow up and who will conclude? Think carefully about what you are aiming for in the negotiation and who of the group is most likely to achieve that aim. It is easy to think that the strongest pair should open the negotiation. Whilst this might be appropriate, it may be more effective to bring them in at a later stage and use negotiators with different strengths—listening, clarifying etc.—at the beginning of the negotiation, when these skills are of key importance.

■ *How much authority?*

How much authority will the negotiators have? In spite of all the planning that has been done, those who carry out the negotiation will need to be given the authority to make decisions at the time. What is the limit of their authority and will it be the same for all those involved? If flexibility is needed over this question, how can the negotiators use the adjournments to clarify their level of authority?

■ *Is everybody happy?*

Do the group members agree on what has been decided and the strategy and tactics to be used? If consensus is being used to reach agreement as opposed to one person deciding what will happen and telling the others that this is so, it is important that each member of the group has been able to contribute his or her opinions and that these have been listened to, even though the eventual outcome may not necessarily reflect their original views. All of the group members must be involved in the decision-making process so that the planning and implementation of the negotiation carries both the individual's commitment and the support of the group. This takes us back to one of the earlier points in this chapter: all of this takes time.

■ The negotiation

The negotiators, i.e those who are negotiating on behalf of the group, may already know the people who are negotiating on behalf of the other party. This can make the early moments of the meeting easier. Whether or not you have met before, some points are fundamental to any meeting.

■ *Be yourself. Be real. Take it easy*

■ *Who is everybody?*

I know that if I'm anxious about a new situation and meeting people for the first time, my brain completely closes down the part that can remember names and faces. Certainly I am introduced to someone whose name is mentioned clearly, but do you think that I can remember it? Not on your life. If I am extremely anxious about a new situation, I spend two-thirds of the rest of the time worrying about forgetting that person's name and trying to remember it, so that I am not giving my full attention to the content of the meeting itself. If a similar thing happens to you, take it easy. See if you can connect in a relaxed way with the person you are meeting and hear their name so that it can enter your brain and remain there. If you haven't heard it the first time, ask them to remind you. If it makes the situation easier, especially where the meeting is quite large, suggest that you put name cards in front of each person to remind you. The main point is to set the theme in a way that will enable the subsequent meeting to be smooth and enjoyable, so clarifying names, positions, roles and so on is important at this stage.

■ *Clarify the agenda and length of the meeting*

Hopefully this should be engrained in your brain by now so that you are sure of the purpose of your meeting, what you are each aiming to get out of it. Once this has been explained by one party, make sure you clarify how much time you are giving to this meeting. Again these are very small points, but they are often overlooked.

Being explicit about timing at the beginning of the meeting makes it easier for everyone to work within that time framework.

■ *Who does what*

The main body of the negotiation should reflect Chapter 6, and the roles you have assigned to those who are negotiating: who will be the main proposer, who will watch for any process or conflict issues, who will come in with specific technical information, and so on. It is useful to have one person who will watch for the need for an adjournment. Whenever you as a group need an opportunity to discuss a point further, suggest adjourning even for a few moments, over a tea break for instance. This will give you an opportunity to reconsider your objectives, check facts, clarify the situation as you each see it and review and plan the next action. Once again you can benefit from having several minds contributing to the same outcome.

Use the tactics mentioned earlier—clarifying, summarising, checking understanding and, most important of all, moving towards a position acceptable to both parties. Clarify, verbally at least, what has been agreed and again follow this up in writing after the meeting. Allow sufficient time—preferably not in the last five minutes before the end of the meeting—to summarise what has been agreed and what remains outstanding.

■ *Stay light*

Remember that even when the going gets tough, and the situation may be hopeless, you don't have to be too solemn.

After the negotiation

As before, review what went well and what needs to be different next time. In your group that planned the negotiation, delight in what went well, especially any success that came as a surprise. Review how far as a group you achieved your aims and objectives.

What has been agreed? During the negotiation were there any surprises, glorious failures or significant information that affected the negotiation process? How might you learn from this in the future? Plan the next step. Allocate the tasks to be done between the members of the group with a date for review and further planning.

11 After the Negotiation

Well done! You managed it. Whether the negotiation took place in person, over the telephone or by letter, it is important to allow yourself some time to reflect on how it went.

This chapter looks at the aftermath, whether it is the end of the negotiation itself or the end of one of the stages in the process. So it also includes a section on adjournment, which can be a highly useful step in the negotiation process.

After the negotiation you may be feeling:

- delighted that it went better than you expected;
- frustrated, dispirited or resigned that it did not come up to your expectations.

Whatever the outcome it is important to do two things. First, celebrate what you did well, and secondly, look at what could have been different to have made the negotiation even more effective. The order in which you do this review is up to you. Some of us find it difficult to focus on what we did well without first getting rid of thoughts and feelings about what we did inadequately, incompetently or whatever. If this is you, allow yourself a few moments to focus on what went wrong, preferably by talking it through with a trusted partner or if not, talking it out to yourself. Obviously it is important to be in a safe place to do this. Speaking out loud helps to clarify our thoughts. If writing is an easier medium for you then use a notebook or piece of paper to jot down your immediate thoughts. Perhaps you are mentally beating yourself up at this stage. The important thing is not to take it too seriously. Sure, you may not have gained what you wanted from the negotiation and while it is important to admit and remedy this, you shouldn't be too critical. Most of us are very good at giving ourselves a hard time for failures, but although it is important to address what went wrong and rectify it, if we focus too much on our sense of inadequacy we will not be operating from a position of strength. Changes need to come from a realistic recognition of our strengths as well as our weaknesses.

The other side of the coin is to look at what went well. If you are pleased with yourself, well done! Congratulate yourself and allow yourself to feel delighted. This is a triumph. You have spent a considerable amount of time and energy in planning for this negotiation and if it went as well as you expected, or better, then this is to be celebrated. Very often at work we do not allow ourselves to feel pleased with work that has gone successfully so do not praise ourselves, let alone praise other people for work that they too have done well. The fact is that we all need praise and if we do not praise ourselves it is difficult to recognise our own worth and therefore to recognise the worth in other people. Celebrating even the smallest thing that we did well begins to build up our own self-worth so that we find it easier to praise others. This becomes an ever-widening circle of strength and possibility.

Use the following exercise as a way of reviewing the negotiation:

What went well? Be as specific as possible and write your responses down. If you can't think of at least two or three things, and for whatever reason are feeling sunk after the negotiation, allow yourself a few moments to feel the awfulness. Then come back to the question and search for even minute aspects that still contributed to the negotiation working well. It may be for instance that you arrived at the meeting on time or that you mentioned what your ideal outcome would be, even though you may not have got it. Think the smallest thoughts. If your list is long, congratulations. Write down all the things that went well before moving on to the next question.

Looking back over the negotiation, what would you do differently next time? (Again write down specific points.) Even if the negotiation went swimmingly, there will always be aspects that could have improved the negotiation even more. Think about these and write them down.

If you have concluded the negotiation, there are still learning points which can carry forward to a similar negotiation in another situation. If you have completed one stage of the negotiation and are meeting again, this review will be more immediate and relevant. Again think specifically and write down what knowledge, information, practice you need before the next encounter. What could you have done more of, less of, stopped doing, or begun? What help will you need in order to make these changes, and who could best provide it?

■■■■■■ Adjournment

If you are to have a further meeting, telephone call or letter with the other party, you are in the glorious position of being in an adjournment. An adjournment is an opportunity to rethink. Negotiation benefits from a climate where two (or more) people can think well enough to identify a solution that will suit all the parties involved. An adjournment contributes well to this outcome and can last for a few minutes, or several hours or days.

As a basic rule, whenever you need time to think, have an adjournment. It has been mentioned earlier in this book, and bears repeating here, that if we are under pressure it is well nigh impossible to think clearly. Thinking clearly is essential in negotiation, so structure the process in a way that will give you this time. On the telephone it is much easier to say, for example: 'That's an interesting suggestion. I need to think about that and check it out with the department. Can I call you back in an hour?' It is a powerful and a logical statement for you are communicating that you need time to consider the suggestion as well as indicating that it is sufficiently important to merit that time.

In a face-to-face meeting, while it is clearly more difficult to take this time out for an adjournment, a number of strategies are available. If a proposal needs further consideration it is still powerful to say something like: 'I need to think about that. Can I call you back tomorrow and let you know? In the meantime we could discuss...'. Obviously there are consequences to taking time out for an adjournment. The bottom line is that, for example, you may lose the contract to a competitor in the intervening time. If you know the other party well you could always say, 'Let's take a break for a few minutes for me to think about that', and then take a walk around the block or visit the women's/men's room. It's surprising where inspiration can strike.

In a letter, the problem of time to think doesn't arise as adjournments are built into the whole process: they are the time in between letters being sent and received.

Use adjournments well. Use them for thinking, reflecting, reassessing and planning the next step. Access other information that is necessary to the next step of the procedure. Practise the skills you require. Ideally, talk the situation through with a listening partner. If you have agreed to get back to the other party by a certain time, make sure that you do even if you haven't a full reply by that time. It will do wonders for your working relationship to make the call you have agreed upon even if it is to say you need another hour or another day. Stick to the agreements you have made.

What has been agreed?

At the end of the meeting or telephone call, clarify and summarise what has been agreed. If the negotiation covered a number of separate issues it is particularly valuable to follow up the conversation with a written letter or memo confirming what was discussed and agreed and in particular who is doing what, by when.

As mentioned earlier, we have selective hearing and can easily forget significant points. Writing down the agreements made will confirm these to both parties, setting out what needs to be done and serving as a springboard for subsequent discussion. This way disparities will be identified. A written note can be valuable later on if the negotiation goes awry, for you can return to those points and recall: 'At our last meeting we agreed that...'.

So as a learning point, whatever has been agreed:

- Confirm it in writing.
- Deliver!

The end

Well done. My aim was that you should feel more enabled, more confident, more informed and attracted to the notion of negotiating either individually or as a member of a group. I hope that this has been achieved and that you will tell me where this book has helped in your negotiation and where it fell down.

This book has been the product of many years and many workshops assisting people to negotiate in the workplace. As such it has been developmental and is still developing. I would be delighted to hear your comments. I can be contacted at BBC Books and in the mean time wish you every success.

Enjoy it!

Bibliography

Recommended further reading

Anne Dickson, *A Woman In Your Own Right—Assertiveness and You*, Quartet, 1982.

Rennie Fritchie and Maggie Melling, *The Business of Assertiveness*, BBC Books, 1991.

Shakti Gawain, *Creative Visualisation*, Bantam, 1979.

Dina Glouberman, *Life Choices and Life Changes through Imagework*, Unwin, 1989.

John Heider, *The Tao of Leadership*, Wildwood House, 1986.

Claire Walmsley, *Assertiveness, the Right to be You*, BBC Books, 1991.

References

The following articles and publications have been referred to in the text:

Robert Eliot, 'Don't sweat the small stuff . . .' etc., *Time Magazine,* 6th June 1983.

J.R.P. French and B. Raven, 'The Bases of Social Power'. pp. 150-167, in D. Cartwright (ed.) *Studies in Social Power,* Ann Arbor, MI: Inst. for Social Research, University of Michigan, 1959.

Rosabeth Moss Kanter, *Men and Women of the Corporation,* Basic Books, 1977.

N. Rackham and J. Carlisle, 'The Effective Negotiator, Parts 1+ 2', *Journal of European Industrial Training,* 2 (6/7), 1978.

B.W. Tuckman and M. A. Jensen, 'Stages of Small Group Development Revisited', *Group and Organisation Studies,* 2, 1977, pp. 419-427.

M. Woodcock and D. Francis, *Organisation Development through Team Building,* Gower, 1982.

BUSINESS MATTERS MANAGEMENT GUIDES

A series of practical self-help book and tape packs bringing tried and tested management techniques to a wide range of people. Each book is accessible and jargon-free and is accompanied by a C50 tape.

MANAGING PRESSURE AT WORK

A practical guide to managing time and other pressures and for coping with stress

Helen Froggatt and Paul Stamp

SPEAK FOR YOURSELF

A practical guide to speaking with confidence

John Campbell

SUCCEED AT YOUR JOB INTERVIEW

A practical guide to being interviewed

George Heaviside

THE BUSINESS OF ASSERTIVENESS

A practical guide to being more effective in the workplace

Rennie Fritchie and Maggie Melling